" This clear mirror of religion,
reflecting nakedly the images of dancers
in combination and separate."

Plate I. Santa Catarina, central part of retable of Cathedral, Goa;
late sixteenth or early seventeenth century.

THE CLEAR MIRROR

A PATTERN OF LIFE IN GOA AND
IN INDIAN TIBET

by

G. EVELYN HUTCHINSON

CAMBRIDGE
AT THE UNIVERSITY PRESS
1936

CAMBRIDGE
UNIVERSITY PRESS

32 Avenue of the Americas, New York NY 10013-2473, USA

Cambridge University Press is part of the University of Cambridge.

It furthers the University's mission by disseminating knowledge in the pursuit of education, learning and research at the highest international levels of excellence.

www.cambridge.org
Information on this title: www.cambridge.org/9781107418950

© Cambridge University Press 1936

First published 1936
First paperback edition 2014

A catalogue record for this publication is available from the British Library

ISBN 978-1-107-41895-0 Paperback

MARGARETAE

uxori amatae

amanter

d.d.

auctor

CONTENTS

PLATES

PREFACE

The places described in this book were visited during the course of the Yale North India Expedition in 1932. The order in which they are discussed is not always that in which they were visited.

The assistance of some of the many people who have helped me is acknowledged in the notes at the end of the book, but others, whose names are unknown to me, cannot therefore be thanked individually. My particular gratitude is due to Mrs Peter of the Moravian Mission in Leh for instructing me in the rudiments of the Tibetan language, and to Dr H. de Terra, leader of the Yale North India Expedition, not only for help and encouragement during the expedition and subsequently, but especially for giving me an opportunity to learn something of the physiographic history of the Indus valley, a subject that his own researches have so brilliantly illuminated.

Any virtue that the following pages may possess is largely due to my wife's critical insight, and I can hardly thank her for the loving care she has expended in the preparation of a somewhat refractory manu-script.

G. E. H.

New Haven, Conn.
25 November 1935

I

SPAIN AT SEA

SPAIN AT SEA

To anyone who has not been there, Spain seems infinitely remote. Kerguelenland can hardly be more distant, St Brandan's Isle more mytho-logical, for the former can be fairly completely explored in a library, and the latter, being wholly imaginary, can be peopled in the mind and studied at will. But Spain might be traversed from one end to the other without anything of the country being discovered. From a distance it seems an essentially Mediterranean land, an aromatic country whose vegetation can be smelt miles out to sea; yet its Mediterraneity does not ally it with the rest of Europe as is the case with Italy, but rather separates. Spain is pictured as a dry remote region, where the intensity of the sun is measured chiefly by the depth of the shadows; a land of crickets and grasshoppers, but, since most of the Iberian species are endemic, of crickets and grasshoppers set apart; a country of archaic politeness and intense dark passions, utterly unhellenic, yet made most comprehensible through the genius of a Cretan painter.

The imagination is most accurately excited by familiar things, which are well enough known to be picked up from a world where they lie at random,

taken apart, reconstructed and redesigned, and their
components put in exact places where they are appropriate. Sit in a café in Paris and look at the reflections
of familiar objects from which whole new worlds can
be constructed. The mirrors on the walls return a
simple, lefthanded version of the righthanded world.
From the shiny surfaces of the cylinders of the coffee
engines a silver vertical world emerges, balanced by a
horizontal world in gold on the brass rails of the bar.
Along the bevelled edges of the window panes small
transverse sections of the passersby run ahead of or
lag behind their possessors; while a final decomposition of the scene is achieved in the glasses and bottles
on the shelves at the side, so that the world of appearances consists now of nothing but fragmentary spots
of light. With these things the imagination may play
undisturbed till it is shocked away from thought to perception by some unwonted thing. Looking up to the
mirrored ceiling, mugs of beer and cups of coffee hang
as if fruits in a tropical orchard. Suddenly wandering
among them is a stupendous animal beauty, her living
body separated from her sculptured head by a violet
and lavender shawl, an earthbrown woman swinging
delicate legs from her immense hips. She has introduced a new startling element into the mental pictures.
An African courtesan, washed up in a Paris street,

has by accident broken the formalistic vision of the mirrors. But that is a rare occurrence; a negress is not often seen in a mirrored ceiling. The Spaniards, however, have made an art of such appearances. They fastened a figure of the Madonna to the surface of a hanging mirror, a cloud of wooden cherubs surrounding her, so that anyone passing by, dissatisfied with an image of the present world, would be rewarded by an apparition of the Queen of Heaven, an illusion of a vision set solidly against unreality. And not content with such a trick on a small scale, Spain has sent out, following not merely her own adventurers but the expanding dominions of Portugal as well, a spiritual army entrusted with placing the Madonna in front of every strange and barbarous culture in which could be recognised the distorted image of her own.

A train rushes south through air from which all moisture was frozen some days before. The atmosphere in the compartment is dampened by the bodies of its occupants, half-a-centimetre of ice forms on the inside of the window panes. Shut off from the world by this ice, the memories of past days struggle with one another. They seem fragments, like bits of painted glass, or perhaps odd tools or clothes thrown into a bag before starting a journey in case some use might be found for them, miscellaneous objects which can be discarded if they prove to be a burden, but which in practice are never thrown away. Daphne in gold, turning not to a green shrub but to a twig of red coral; catfish swimming under the ice on the little aquaria outside the animal shops along the river front; the tapestries of the Lady and the Unicorn. The Virgin on her mirror struggles with the harlot negress in hers, now blending, now antagonists, each triumphing for a moment. A man snores in the corner opposite, a rug slips; sleep that had come to the mind moves away a little, mocking. Wakeful legs are pushed at random through the cold air of the carriage. Then the hypnotic rattling of the train dominates, sleep again approaches, now coming first to the limbs, leaving the catfishes swimming for a while round Daphne's frozen coral. But at last they die in the cold of an emptied mind; the Virgin stares woodenly from her mirror into the dark; the negress has found a new lover. The train rattles to its unconscious passengers.[1]*

In the morning the train, emerging from the cold night that lay over Provence, reaches Marseilles. The city, made of wharfs, white walls, green shutters and red roofs, seems to have been thrown up by the sea. Whatever may formerly have occupied its ancient site

* Numerals in the text refer to notes at the end.

is now buried. The process of burial still continues. A brand new cathedral has been deposited there; the old cathedral, outgrown and discarded, lies by its side, far below the level of the street. Under this small sanctuary Lazarus is reputed to lie. He came to France with his sisters and their black servant St Sarah, whom the gypsies venerate at Les-Saintes-Maries-de-la-Mer. By the side of his second and perennial tomb, children are repeating their catechism. A priest is instructing the boys, and several middle-aged ladies have classes of little girls grouped around them. One of these children, whose hair is golden-red and whose grey-green eyes, set in a pale ivory face, seem to have seen the whole of human existence, repeats to her teacher, "Les sept péchés mortels sont...." The traditions of the land have burrowed underground in Marseilles; the city above has been built and nourished by the sea and is perpetually fluid. People come here merely to leave again. The best food is obtained from the sea, langouste and numerous kinds of fishes; bread and potatoes must here be saturated with the marine flavours of such sea-beasts if they are fully to be enjoyed. Notre-Dame-de-la-Garde, standing on a hill that towers over the anadyomenous growth of the city, is the only church in Marseilles that has come fully into the open, but it is a marine church paid for by the sea and filled with votive models of ships. Recently a smart red monoplane has been added to the collec-tion by the devoted mother of some aeronaut. It hangs in readiness at the end of the nave. Notre-Dame-de-la-Garde has had in these days to assume new duties; it is too soon to know where they may take her.

Three Jesuit fathers from Barcelona have come to Marseilles to stay but for a moment. Their society has met with new difficulties in its ancient home and its members are taking refuge in its professed houses in Africa, South America and Asia. These three are perhaps the last from Spain to embellish the mirror in which India reflects the Mediterranean and the Medi-terranean lands reflect India. At Marseilles the fathers embark for Bombay; at the height of Spanish mis-sionary fervour in the sixteenth and seventeenth cen-turies, Goa would have been their destination; even to-day the stewards on the boat are mostly Goanese.

The boat passes Stromboli; passengers, speculating on the islet volcano, suspect it is Vesuvius or contest that it is Etna. Dolphins leap through the gilded crests of grey-blue waves, and talk turns to flying fishes and sharks. The Jesuit fathers stand apart from the other passengers, taking pictures of the islands with a small hand-camera; then they walk up and down with their breviaries. Later in the morning, one of the fathers sits on deck, sorting loose photographs and putting them in an album. The collection forms his complete illustrated biography. First come his father and mother, his brother in the Spanish army, then school groups, football teams in shorts and sweaters, "les jours héroïques", he explains, the long laboratories of his college, portraits of students, and geological parties examining barren exposures of tilted limestone. And, mixed with these, set in the middle of many of the pages of the album, surrounded by the schoolboys in football shorts and the students in laboratories, smiles Mary, the Queen of Heaven and the lady of his heart.

In the evening the ship glides through the Straits of Messina. Behind the rows of street lights, the hills rise faintly black against the sky. Between the front streets and the bottom of the slope a marionette theatre no doubt still stands; the performance will have just begun. The stage is filling with figures so heroic that a live man, appearing at the side of them, would suddenly seem transformed to more than a giant relative to the four feet of painted wooden immensity supported by a rod from above. But the ghost of Orlando does not trouble Charybdis; the lights of the broken town alone evoke memories of his puppet. The boat moves toward the darkness east of Taormina.

The photographs of college laboratories in the album

turn conversation toward science. The nearness of Sicily deflects it to one of the most curious products of the impact of scientific knowledge upon religious logic, the *Embryologia Sacra* of Francesco-Emanuele Cagniamila.[2] This book, the work of an eighteenth-century Sicilian priest, is a discussion of, almost propaganda for, the immediate Caesarian section of dead expectant mothers, that their unborn children may be baptised and so brought to salvation. In order that priests and others, not familiar with embryological anatomy, may administer this sacrament correctly, elaborate instructions are given, the method of baptism of very young embryos being carefully described. It being doubtful, writes Cagniamila, to what extent the embryonic membranes are to be considered part of the embryo, and therefore capable of receiving the sacrament of baptism, they should be opened so as to expose the embryo whenever this can be done without undue risk. In dealing with very young embryos, however, the best procedure is to give a conditional baptism to the membranes, using the formula, "Si tu es capax, ego te baptiso"; then, on opening the membranes, the baptism should be repeated in the conditional form, "Si tu es capax et si non es baptisatus." By this method it is possible to avoid the indignities of attempting to baptise what is unbaptisable on the one hand or what has already been baptised on the other; every chance, however, is taken to save the foetal soul. The baptism may be performed by immersion in a plate or glass of water. A note added in a French edition of the book, apparently by the translator, suggests that the water should have the chill taken off. The priest need not fear that he is drowning the embryo, for in the womb the latter "swims there in a certain liquid with which the first membrane is filled".

Cagniamila also considers monstrous births, conjoint twins and the like. If a monster should lack a head entirely, it is by no means certain that it possesses a rational soul, and it should be baptised conditionally. The mere lack of eyes or nose, however, does not imply the acephalic condition, and in such cases baptism may be unconditional. If a normal human head is joined to an animal body, "as has happened several times", the monster is of very dubious origin and nature, and should be baptised conditionally. Double monsters like the Siamese twins are to be given separate baptism for each individual, but good authority exists for the plural form "ego vos baptiso" in urgent cases. If a more intimate fusion occurs, one head should be baptised unconditionally, the other, preferably the smaller less perfect one, conditionally. The baptism of the seven-headed monster born at Novara in 1587 must have been an elaborate affair if all the heads were brought to salvation.

Taking such doctrines from Spain as part of its cargo, perhaps for the last time, the boat leaves the Sicilian lights and heads toward Egypt. Then, through succeeding nights and days, it pushes between the tracts of desert that still limit the familiar world. Beyond them, the Indian Ocean lies, reflecting by day the pale grey-blue of a pale grey-blue cardboard sky, from which at night all colour fades rapidly. Only the horizontal light of sunset and sunrise can gild its undulant waters, so that then only they seem fit to receive the flying fish as they dart back into the waves or flip their crests with propulsive tails. At such times the sea might have borne

"The Andalusian merchant, that returns
Laden with cochineal and china dishes",[3]

and still might be the home of mermen and sirens, or of the fabled fish in the form of a bishop that the learned Rondeletius[4] described but could never obtain. In such lights, the islands that fringe the long low Malabar coast might be inhabited by the most fantastic monsters, countries of hermaphrodites or double twins beneath the palm trees, beings whose strange bodies would of necessity have given birth to the most extraordinary customs. And beyond the islands might be found the colony of surpassingly beautiful courtesans, whom travellers have reported from hearsay as descended from a whole convent of fallen nuns. If any men have visited them, they have not cared to substantiate the story. But, as the tropical night so quickly approaches, these dreams must fade. The fish in the circumambient ocean slough off the picturesque skins that the mediaeval artists fashioned for them, and take on their natural shapes. Rapidly their forms pass through centuries of knowledge until the time, when Bloch,[4] *Ichthyologorum facile princeps*, published his great monument of zoological iconography, and when they become related scale to scale, fin ray to fin ray, with the fish of the mind. Then the water darkens; the superb colours of Bloch's pages are hidden. All the learning, all the knowledge, that man has sought out, seem to have stolen with the dying sun into the deserts of Arabia.

Not until morning are these wonders remembered again. Then, though the ship irrevocably reaches the sunraped slums of Bombay, the islands of the coast, though now faded, are known never to have been merely a dream. Close at hand, on Elephanta, the gods of India, once alarmed by a Portuguese bombardment, have remained hidden in their underground temples. Not far south, on the Island of Goa,[5] the mirrors that the Jesuits set up still reflect the Mediterranean lands, though, as in the speculum of a telescope turned to a distant star, the events that are reflected in these mirrors have happened long ago.

In the cathedral of Velha Goa,[6] the canons have sung the morning office. Three priests vested for mass and two acolytes in red cassocks enter the cathedral from the sacristy and cross to the chapel in front of which the canons have been singing. An elegant young man wanders down the nave, disappears and appears again in the small organ loft above the choir. Over the altar of the chapel, Saint Sebastian stands, his left arm tied in benediction against a tree. Two turbaned but white-faced archers crouch on either side of him, martyring him with imaginary arrows, while above a cherub holds a circle of gold in readiness to welcome him to heaven. The incense has been lit and its smoke rises as the altar is censed. The sun that passes at the sides of Saint Sebastian is caught by the rising smoke.

The canons stand in the tall white aisle of the empty church, grouped round a lectern. In the middle, one beats time; another points with a rod to the immense black notes on the page open before them. It is the feast of the Presentation, and they are beginning to sing. But the beating of one rod and the pointing of another make little difference to them. The rich plain-song of the Gloria is beyond them; what they sing is irrespective of the notes in the missal and bears no relation to the accompaniment of the elegant youth at the organ. So the labours of the Magister Cantorum are wasted, but perhaps that does not matter, for the Presentation is not an important feast.

A beautifully formed and almost naked man, dark-chocolate coloured, wanders into the cathedral with a bottle of turpentine or oil, going from chapel to chapel as though he were trying to remove some spots of paint that he cannot find. Then, as the canons begin to affirm their faith with voices that wander far and irregularly from the path laid down by the notes of the missal, a procession of half-a-dozen partly clothed women enters the south transept, gay red and white cottons wound tightly about their hips and held in front by the strings of beads round their necks. They walk slowly across the transepts, carrying on their heads huge candlesticks, two pastoral staffs and several silvery metal crowns, which they take through the sacristy door in the north transept.

The celebration of the mass has proceeded to the gospel. The faces of the standing canons seem black against the white walls of the church and then white above the black of their cassocks. But, looking from one to the other, each face varies from another in its blackness and whiteness.

In four days' time is the feast of Saint Catherine; the church is being cleaned on her account. She stands on the immense retable in the choir, hidden from the black and white canons by the piers of the nave. She is golden, and, while mass is sung, six lighted candles illuminate her. At the sides of the retable, her life and death are depicted. She is disputing with the pagan sages of the Emperor Maximinus, is delivered from the torturing wheel, beheaded by soldiers and her body laid in a tomb by angels while her head is caught up to heaven in a cloth. Schoolmen may profitably have discussed this miracle, for, if her body remains on earth till the judgment, it may be asked if her head lies inactive in heaven awaiting the last day for its material though glorified body, or if it is provided with some temporary trunk of celestial matter till the resurrection of the golden body that we see lain in the tomb, or if she has joined the saints with a glorified material head attached to a purely spiritual body. Catherine herself, untroubled by this problem of celestial anatomy, stands between Corinthian columns in the middle of the retable on the prostrate body of the emperor, whose head she has transfixed with her sword, guarding her secret and unperplexed by earthly disputations. Meanwhile, a greater miracle has occurred at the feet of Saint Sebastian; the word made flesh has taken on the accidents of bread and wine. A small shrill bell rings; then the deep bell in the roof is tolled three times, and after each of its notes a small charge of powder is exploded outside the church. But coconut palms alone stand to bow their heads if a breeze should chance to blow at the moment, and only the wooden saints in the neigh-bouring churches have hands raised in adoration.

Saint Ignatius Loyola stands on the retable in the Bom-Jesus[7] on the other side of the deserted square. His church is far richer but much less beautiful than Saint Catherine's cathedral. The façade, the only one of stone now surviving intact in old Goa, is a typical monument to the power of the Jesuits, whereas that of the cathedral simply and convincingly shows that man can create form and rhythm from stucco and whitewash. Saint Ignatius himself is golden like Saint Catherine, but, lacking her beauty, he stands immense, ecstatic and rather ridiculous. He has set his eyes on heavenly things, so that his beard points down the church and his halo begins to fall off his head behind. The very lack of meaning in the ostentation of the carved and gilded wood around him proclaims that earthly form has been transcended in his blessed vision. Below him in the south transept, in a silver shrine, sleeps his greatest disciple, Francis Xavier. "In everything he is a contrast to us here, and many high folks think it was imprudent to send such a man here whose manner of living is scandalous. They say the white people will be despised by the natives, if they act in the same fashion, for the natives like splendour and magnificence in their conquerors, and we ought to impress upon them that we are a superior race, not mere hewers of wood and drawers of water as they."[8]

To the west of the Jesuitic façade of the Bom-Jesus, on the slopes of a little hill, lies the Convent of Saint Monica,[9] the largest religious house in Goa, and once the second largest in the whole of the dominions of Portugal. The convent is built about a huge garden court, round which there are three storeys of cloisters. The main door of the church faces a square; above it is a storey of windows, and again above them an elaborate pediment, flanked on either side by a balustrade. Like all the more important buildings surviving in old Goa, the convent was built after the disastrous Spanish domination of Portugal in the last quarter of the sixteenth century, and, as in the case of the other buildings, there is nothing specifically Portuguese in its construction.[10] The white stucco and the pediments of both the convent and the cathedral give these buildings a curious resemblance to South African houses of the late seventeenth century and the eighteenth century. It seems possible that the suitability of such a style to a warm climate may have impressed itself on the Dutch in their Spanish wars of the seventeenth century, in which the Portuguese colonies were involved, and in which many Indian slaves, some perhaps expert stucco workers, were carried off to the Cape of Good Hope.

In her niche in the centre of this charming white façade, Saint Monica stands in prayer, facing a square littered with stones and surrounded with broken buildings. On the retable of the church of the convent, she stands again in prayer, looking at the great iron grille behind which a hundred nuns once assembled to hear mass. The three explosions may divert her mind momentarily to the cathedral, but other miracles have occurred nearer at hand.

High on the wall of the church, in a small gallery, is suspended a crucifix hidden by a crimson curtain. At the sides of the gallery, like immense earrings of elaborately worked silver wire, hang two lamps bearing pelicans that have plucked the stones from their once jewelled breasts; from a third lamp in front, the pelicans would seem to have flown away with their booty. The lamps are always lighted; a special fund to keep them burning has survived the suppression of the religious orders in 1834, and all the other vicissitudes of the convent; so that in the now deserted church, three small flames perennially hang around the crimson curtain. In the early days of the convent, the figure on the crucifix, now so tenderly covered, moved its eyes on several occasions, as is attested by the apostolic inquisitors who were called in to examine the miraculous phenomenon. After one of these manifestations, the cross was also found to have grown one palm in length. There is a geography of miracles, no less than of animals and plants. In Naples, not merely does the blood of Saint Januarius liquefy before great crowds twice a year, but, hidden in the treasuries of Neapolitan churches, are small samples from the veins of other saints, among them Saint Stephen at Santa Chiara, and Saint Luigi Gonzaga at the old Jesuit church; these also have their appropriate festivals for unclotting. At Ravello, the blood of Saint Pantaleo behaves in a like way. That another Goan crucifix, now in the chapel almost opposite that of Saint Sebastian in the cathedral, should have shown a still greater capacity for growth, increasing at some unspecified time by as much as four palms in length, should not therefore be considered surprising.

The gallery around which the silver lamps are hanging can be entered from the upper floor of the three-storeyed cloisters. For a short space on either side of the door the walls have been decorated with mural paintings. Since the crucifix was not moved from the main choir of the church till 1636, when it was miraculously preserved from destruction by fire, it may be concluded that the paintings were probably executed about this date, and it is quite certain that they are not earlier. They are undoubtedly the work of a local copyist who had been supplied with European models; side by side is found a row of small decorative figures of saints and armoured archangels in the manner of the Italian renaissance, and, immediately outside them, scenes of the Passion which appear to be coloured copies of Flemish or German wood engravings. In these Passion scenes, much of the formality of mediaeval painting has survived, so that on the plaster of this wall, the Middle Ages and the modern world seem to be left struggling long after the battle has been decided in Europe.[11]

To-day the church is deserted, but once a year the miraculous crucifix has power to fill it, though the nuns have gone and their garden in the cloister court is no longer fruitful. But, under the quiet shades of lemon and orange trees, in groves of papaya, banana and mango, from the fruits of which the inmates of the convent prepared once celebrated preserves, not only crucifixes were miraculous, for a dying nun, Sister Maria de Jesus, herself displayed the bleeding stigmata of the cross. A large picture in the convent shows her lying in state. The painter has arranged all the funerary candles behind her body so as not to obscure our view of her hands and feet, which show the wounds conspicuously, while a discreet aperture in her habit, placed high up on her right shoulder, even allows a sight of her fifth stigma. No echo of the feats of the baroque sanctity of Europe has troubled her long-drawn Gothic tranquility. The style of her holiness belongs to an earlier day, before saints floated in the flesh above the altar,[12] perching high in conventual churches of Calabria, rivalling the supernatural little figures hung around the Christmas crib as models for the gigantic visions of Solimena. But the simple miracle of this nun is well authenticated, for the authorities are stated to have attempted unsuccessfully to wash with soap, salt and vinegar, the wounds from her dead body, which was, in response to popular insistence, borne in procession through the city.

Around the square on which the convent faces are

Plate II. The Flagellation, upper cloister of S. Monica, Goa; 1636 or later.

Plate III. Pulpit of church of S. Pedro, Panelim, Goa; sixteenth to seventeenth century.

broken buildings. On the west side, the Hospital of Saint John of God now consists of little but a ruined church, an entrance hall containing a curious rough painting of the Last Judgment, and a well-preserved privy. Opposite, the monastery of Saint Augustine has retained only its ruined church, the façade of which has but recently fallen.

Far away toward the modern town of Panjim, on the east side of the thicket which represents the great Jesuit College of Saint Roch, Saint Peter stolidly clutches the keys of heaven and hell, as the sunlight filters in through a small window behind the gilded reredos of his church. Against the north wall of the nave is fixed a pulpit, supported by carved mermaids who seem to swim out into the air, as if they were the figureheads of ships, carrying the Faith from the gates of Goa to all the seaports of Asia. Each holds in her mouth a bunch of grapes from the true vine and refreshes our eyes with her swelling belly and breasts. High on the wall above the pulpit, and dark with age, hangs a picture[13] very different from the murals around the door to the miraculous crucifix, a picture in which the modern world of Europe is developing from, rather than in conflict with, the old. It repre-sents that most rhythmical of subjects, the Deposition, and is perhaps of the Netherlandish school of Portuguese painting. The angular rhythm of the pale body of Christ, accentuated by the disposition of masses of dull red in the drapery, is essentially mediaeval, but the faces, in spite of their tranquility, suggest that pre-occupation with the physiognomy of emotional expression which, in northern painting, is the most characteristic symptom of the awakening of man's curiosity. This little work is no doubt the most perfect painting now in existence in Goa. A Magdalene in the Bom-Jesus, covering her naked breasts with her hair, is seated beside a small goblet, below which is inscribed, "Fulcite me floribus, stipate me malis, quia amore langueo." The picture is locally attributed to Murillo, and by some even to Raphael. In its present state, the general impression is a *fin-de-siècle* advertisement for a hair restorative; the over-painting is such that it may cover anything. But, in the cathedral, over the altar of the chapel of Our Lady of Sorrows, in the north transept, half-covered by a gangrenous crucifix of later date, is a picture which, though certainly an Indian copy, conveys a more lasting impression than any of the other Goanese altar pieces. As far as can be seen, it represents the Last Judgment. The main figure visible is an angel in white and red, assisting a soul upwards from the bottom of the picture; on his right, another angel is encouraging two

souls by an upward gesture; the damned are relegated
to the extreme left, where a small angel in the distance
is threatening them with a sword. The top part of the
painting is covered, so that it is impossible to see the
figure of the Supreme Judge. A small attendant angel
in a very cold pale blue robe floats on a cloud, and
now alone represents the panoply of heaven in the
upper part of the painting. The painter responsible
for this work was undoubtedly Indian for, in the very
accentuated noses of the profile figures at the bottom
of the painting, we catch an echo of so many Indian
miniatures. But the picture, though so poor a copy,
persistently asks how an Indian copyist would proceed
if he had to copy an El Greco. Would the pale blue
of the little angel's robe have remained essentially intact, while the fabulous pink of the garment of the
larger angel became a commonplace red ? The spacing
of the figures would no doubt remain unchanged;
even the obscurity of the angel damning the lost souls,
whose position far over to the edge implies a pre-
occupation with heavenly things, and at the same
time suggests unlimited distance behind the picture
plane, might remain. But could the broken clouds
of El Greco's all-pervading atmosphere solidify to anything as dough-like as in this picture ? Would the
full-faced portraits retain a trace of the original, while

great false noses had been added to the profiles? This may be an idle fancy, but it is impossible when seeing the painting for the last time not to think that once there was in Goa a painting of some importance of the Last Judgment, whoever may have painted it, and to wonder somewhat hopelessly if the original may not be under the paint which can be seen today.

Mass in the cathedral is now ended. The Theatine church opposite, tenanted only by a few bats and a broad-leaved plant sprouting from a cornice inside its dome, has been locked some time.

To the east, a thick grove of coconut palms covers the site of the monastery of the Dominicans,[14] whose church was the most splendid of all in Goa. Its magnificent façade stood at the top of a high flight of steps. The pillars of the choir were washed with gold and the walls adorned with pictures illustrating the martyrology of the order. Nearby, behind an open space on which horses were trained, there was a chapel dedicated to Saint John the Baptist, a delicate aquatic sanctuary, curiously ornamented with shells, and sup-plied with water from a neighbouring fountain. A little to the north a stucco façade with a flat pediment marks the position of the church of the Carmelite Convent, where the canonisation of Saint Theresa was made the occasion of a great celebration on

20 May 1623. Two youths in travelling costume were sent on horseback to bring the news to the viceroy, announcing their message in verse. At a pageant in the evening, an image of the saint was exhibited, surrounded by twelve persons bearing devices and mottoes in various languages. The city was illuminated and a masquerade held. Pietro della Valle, an Italian traveller who had known the saint personally, appeared dressed as an Arab of the desert.

Now the canons disappear from the cathedral and the churches are shut as the morning heat increases. Only the church of Saint Francis,[15] pointing its eastern end against the western High Altar of the cathedral, still has open doors. Its walls complete the fragmentary story of pictorial art in old Goa. On either side of each arch above the chapels of the nave, angels in long stripy robes are painted; these figures alone suggest that the church stands on Indian soil. But, in the choir, the oriental angels and the arabesques around them give place to a set of entirely Europeanised paintings, probably the last to be executed in any Goan church. In a double vertical row on panels, stretching up from the floor to the vault on either side, the lives of Saint Francis and his disciples have been illustrated. As a repentant young rake, he is kneeling before the crucifix on an altar, dressed in a red coat and knee breeches. His stockings look silken and have elaborate clocks; his shoes are black with red heels. He kneels in a stiff mediaeval pose, his oval long-nosed face curiously reminiscent of Saint Mary Magdalene in the *pietà* at S. Pedro. He receives from the crucifix the miraculous command to rebuild the Church. In a later scene, he is changing his red coat for a brown habit, and in the following pictures the well-known incidents of the later life of the saint are given. In one, he is receiving the Pope's permission to found his order; in another, preaching at the Saracen court; in another, receiving the stigmata. The costumes, particularly that of the youthful repentant Francis, show the picture to be of late seventeenth-century date, yet it was painted by someone quite out of touch with contemporary European art, who developed such ability as he may have possessed by a study of reproductions of much earlier European pictures, that were quite innocent of any baroque elements of design.

Christian art in Goa, whether at its best as in the architecture of the cathedral and a few pieces of wood sculpture,[16] or, as in the case of the paintings, merely derivative, curious and dull, is almost completely European, and has taken nothing from the east but a few angels and the drawing of a few artificial

Plate IV. Saint Francis of Assisi as a penitent young man; choir of church of S. Francisco, Goa; late seventeenth century.

Plate V. Temple at Mardol; seventeenth century.

moustaches and artificial noses; but it has given more
than is usually suspected to the surrounding country.
The Hindu architecture of Portuguese India has been
most violently influenced by the invaders. Inland and
to the south-east of the hardly separated island on
which the old Portuguese city stands, is a group of
populous villages around Hindu temples that enjoy
a considerable local reputation. These temples are
built in a style of almost completely classical deriva-
tion. If some eighteenth-century English nobleman,
ignorant of Indian architecture though well-travelled
in Europe, had desired an Indian villa and had been
anxious not to construct anything too out of harmony
with his Palladian residence nearby, he would doubtless have built something very similar to these temples
at Manyesha and Mardol, Bandordem and Ponda.
Only the high-pitched roofs of some of them seem out
of harmony with such a fancy. Perhaps the Manyesha
temple alone has preserved something of its original
precincts; it is set back some distance from the road
that leads from Goa to Ponda.[17] A restrained baroque
gateway, bearing a Sanskrit inscription,[18] gives access
to a long avenue of palm trees. This avenue runs along
the side of a tank, the back wall of which forms a
curved pediment; under the pediment, bathing steps
run down from the temple to the water. The other

temples lie too near to the present streets to have retained such elaborate entrances, if they ever possessed
them, although close to the Bandordem temple is
a pretty garden with a dovecote and a small palace,
crudely decorated with paintings of Portuguese soldiers.

Each temple stands within a residential court, and
is entered through a porch with its own pointed roof.
This porch leads into a hall with a high roof; sometimes there are other porches or entrances at the sides
of the hall. The temple at Bandordem, near Ponda,
has a series of grotesque earthenware animals along
the angle of the roof, that gives it an intimate and
frivolous aspect, and that would well accord with the
eighteenth-century passion for chinoiserie. In front of
the principal doors of the Manyesha and Mardol
temples, there are tall towers whose classical capitals
are elegantly constructed of stucco; an unfinished
tower at Mardol has particularly ambitious Corinthian
pilasters. At the far end of the central hall stands a
domed sanctuary, surrounded by an ambulatory and
containing the principal image. Inside, the main halls
are predominantly light blue, and have flat ceilings
hung with witch balls, inverted bell glasses and
numberless cut-glass chandeliers. A niche on either
side of the sanctuary doors contains a figure of a god
which, if it had been in the oriental villa of a dilettante

and not in India, would have been imported from the East at great expense and have become the object of much admiration and envious gossip. There are a few lotus-carved capitals and occasional crude stone reliefs set into the walls. A girl comes in, wearing a purple sari and with orange blossoms in her black hair, touching the clapper of a suspended bell as she enters. Priests in their loin cloths move mysteriously about the image of the god in the dark-domed sanc-tuary, where little lights are flickering. But these things merely serve to show that the dilettante has played his game with perfect skill. They appear in these temples, not as part of the life of the land, but rather as an additional and expensive affectation on the part of an eccentric.

Such a fancy, though well expressing the mood that these curious buildings evoke, is hardly historical; at least one of the temples was standing at the end of the seventeenth century, when the mottled day of eccen-tricity had scarcely begun its dawn. Gemelli Careri, an Italian traveller, visited Mardol in 1695 on his way to Ponda, the first stage of a journey from Goa to the camp of the Great Mogul at Galgala. After con-suming a Jacca fruit, so large that a man could scarce carry it, Careri examined the "famous *Pagod*" at Mardol. "The way into the Court is over a covered

Bridge of three Arches, up to which there are two Staircases. On the right of this Court is an octan-gular Structure, consisting of seven Rounds of small Columns, with handsome Capitals, and little Win-dows in the Intervals, one of which serves for a Door. They say this was Built to put Lights in on the Festivals of their Idols, as was the other place, like it, on the left, not yet finished." The covered bridge has dis-appeared, but both towers are standing, just as Careri saw them; one is still unfinished.

This temple cannot have been built long after the construction of the churches in the European city. The domes of all the temples, save that at Bandordem, are so European that they must have been built by Western architects, or more probably have been copied from one of the newly constructed churches. The Theatine church, whose dome is the only one to sur-vive in old Goa, naturally suggests itself; Careri says that its design was based on S. Andrea della Valle in Rome. But other domes formerly existed in the vicinity, for Cottineau de Kloguen writes of the seminary of Chorão, on the island of that name, "Behind the house is a small chapel, with an elegant dome, and Grecian pillars supporting the edifice, giving the whole from a distance, the true appearance of a scenery of Greece." Cottineau, although he wrote

Plate VI. Towers in front of temple at Mardol; seventeenth century.

Plate VII. Temple at Bandordem; probably seventeenth century.

A Geographical Compendium for the Use of Schools; being an accurate description of all the empires, kingdoms, republics and states in the known world.... The whole arranged in catechical form, Baltimore 1806, does not seem to have set eyes on the sceneries of Greece.

Whether or not the inspiration for these buildings was ultimately derived from an existing Roman structure, or from some building in an imagined Greece, the style was affected so perfectly that only on leaving the temple courts for the populous little bazaars of the adjacent villages, through which large motor buses crowded with pilgrims pass on their way to the baroque gates, is it clear that the classical and Christian style is the alien mode of expression in this country. While these villages around Ponda prosper, in the ancient capital two or three tiny shops selling coconut milk represent the former centre of European commercial expansion in the East.

On 25 November 1510, the Feast of Saint Catherine of Alexandria, the renowned Afonso d'Albuquerque captured Goa from the "Moors" and restored it to Portugal. Each year, on a few such festivals, the old town is given back to Christendom; for a few hours the palm trees share their dominion with a crowd that arrives by small boats and motor buses.

The cathedral has been cleaned and some new

H   33   3

marble paving stones set at the beginning of the choir. For several days an immense bamboo ladder has been pulled about the nave. From the top of this, a man climbs over the whitewashed cornices above the piers, and sets in place red and yellow hangings. As each section of the church is decorated, the swaying ladder is pulled to the next by a man and a woman at the bottom. To bring it round the corner of a pier into the main nave from a transept, the climber must ascend and, standing on the cornice with a rope, swing the top of the ladder clear of the corner as the man and woman move its foot. The women who were carrying the candlesticks in procession, to be stored in the sacristy, now spend hours with cleansing bricks on the floor of the choir. At their side, a few naked children play on the newly cleaned marble. Outside in the square, little booths are set up; tables, chairs and provisions are brought, so that on the morning of the festival the old town is better supplied with restaurants than any other place in Portuguese India. The booths will be kept standing till over the feast of Saint Francis Xavier on 3 December, and, mixed with them, there are others where ex votos, heads, arms and children, modelled in wax, are sold, but for Saint Catherine these do no trade. The saint in the silver shrine is more powerful than the lady on the golden retable.

On the day of her feast, the military officials in dark blue and red come in cars early in the morning to do Saint Catherine honour, and wait aimlessly on the edge of the crowd outside the cathedral. Here they are joined by a solitary representative of what was once the greatest navy afloat, a captain without a ship, now solely in charge of the harbour. Finally, the governor himself comes in a large car, and the officers, becoming rather less aimless, salute him and follow him to inspect a company of newly enlisted recruits, who have just arrived by water from the new city of Panjim. After the inspection, the governor goes to adore the Sacrament, somewhat perfunctorily, while the crowd flows into the church. The men are all wearing European clothes and carry the soft black hats which are worn in all Mediterranean countries. The women show greater diversity, more social distinction and a more traditional mode in their costumes. The peasants who, with bare backs and legs, were a day or two since scrubbing the floor of the choir, are now enveloped from head to foot in the finest wool; they stand in the nave in groups, so that they seem to be dark virgin martyrs about to join the choir of the saints. Among them are more prosperous country women in long wide dresses of black taffeta, their hair covered with little black lace headdresses. Their daughters wear the same black headdresses, but their taffeta frocks are pink or white. A family crowds into a carved pulpit in the nave, which, as it is unused to-day, provides a point of vantage from which to hear the service and observe the crowd. The mother is about forty, her aristocratic face seems stained with walnut juice, finely modelled, worn, practical and not without humour. She glances through spectacles perched on her long nose at her service-book, turns to keep two small children in order, or to admire her thirteen-year-old daughter who is sucking at a fan in a listless charming mood; then she fingers her rosary and whispers to a friend. Perched in their bracket of pale carved wood, they seem like a Neapolitan ice composed of white, pink and dark cream spilling over an elaborate wafer cone. And, mixed with these, some grouped as a choir of saints, others as confectionery, are a few girls, élégantes from the New City, with wide hats and flowery chiffon trailing on the floor.

If now time is reversed in the mind, the small lace kerchiefs on the heads of the countrywomen grow as they recede from the present till they are transformed into their ancestors, the crêpe mantos that enveloped the great ladies attending this festival for the first time in the newly finished cathedral.[19] These ladies, kept rigidly secluded, only ventured to church for such an

important feast. A palanquin was set down at the
door of the cathedral; slowly two gentlemen of her
entourage assisted the fidalga to her feet. Beneath the
fine translucent crêpe of her manto, the cloth of gold
of her skirt sparkled in the powerful sun beneath the
white wall of the façade, so that for a moment the
vision of the golden saint surrounded by a blaze of
candles, set deep in the dark of the church, was
eclipsed. Rubies and emeralds jangling against pearls
turned back the fiercest rays that reached them; while
the deep burning eyes of the lady set fire to her cheeks
so that they seemed rouged with glowing powdered
charcoal. Once within the door, the black haze
closed around her for the church was darkened by its
windows, filled with mother-of-pearl instead of glass,
and this darkness was relieved only by the great gold
rosary that she fingered as one of her attendants fetched
her holy water. The lady's shoes covered but the tips
of her toes and raised her six inches from the floor.
These shoes were of the Venetian kind called chopines,
but they did not aspire to the extravagant heights of
those worn by the ladies of Venice, where a whole
treatise was published on the mode of wearing them
and where theologians attacked them as impediments
to kneeling in church, or defended them as a limitation
to excessive dancing. There the women who followed

this ligneous fashion, must have seemed like images carried in procession, towering several feet above the heads of the crowd, but even here, though supported by two attendants without whom she could not have walked, it took the lady a quarter of an hour to reach the centre of the nave. Her servants therefore had ample time to make her place in the church ready, bringing a rich Persian carpet and an embroidered mattress on which was set a gilded Chinese chair; they stood waiting with her fan, handkerchief and a devotional book, should she have required them. Behind the lady walked a number of slave girls, an anthropological collection of beauty culled from all over the Peninsula of India. There were also free Portu-guese women servants, who, as their mistress that day was with them in church, must avert their eyes from those of their lovers in the crowd under the great white vault. This crowd of common people milled around the chapel where the Sacrament was reserved, so that the shuffle of the fantastic shoes of the great ladies was for a moment lost in the general murmur of movement, and these exalted beings of black and gold, leading little processions slowly to their chosen places, seemed to belong to another world, which though using the same space as the inhabitants of the familiar universe, moved quite differently in time, a

few minutes of their lives seeming to occupy hours.
But such a development of the vision throws too great
a strain on the imagination, and, as in waking from
a dream, some slow rhythmic movement becomes
accelerated till it is found to be the ticking of a watch,
so the mantos shorten until their black lace covers the
heads of a few countrywomen who are climbing into
an unused pulpit, and the slow shuffling sound of the
ladies, heard again approaching through the crowd,
is quickened into the sharp click of high heels as three
of the élégantes arrive from the New City. Only the
saints at the back of the church, their white robes
hiding the muscles of their dark limbs, remain unchanged as the vision passes.

Above the heads of the congregation, silver crosses
begin to sway as the priests that bear them take their
places in the main aisle of the nave. They face toward
the main door, and, behind them at the crossing of
the transept, stands a priest with a reliquary, in which
is a minute fragment of the golden body which the
angels of the retable are laying in a golden tomb. The
crosses sway again, and the procession leaves the
church, cross bearers, the relic and its attendants, the
governor, the military officials, the police, and the
captain of the harbour in his cocked hat. They disappear round the north side of the church, and, passing

the Franciscan convent, stop at the tiny chapel of Saint
Catherine on the site dedicated by Albuquerque to
the patroness of the city. On their return to the south
side, small charges of powder explode continually as
the relic passes; they are set off by men at the edge of
the path, but the spectators, moving forward with the
procession, hide them, so that the powder seems to
discharge spontaneously. The procession enters the
cathedral and disperses; the spectators outside follow
the relic and join the large congregation already collected in the nave.

A new movement is seen at the main door; a new
procession arrives. The aged archbishop of Goa is
coming up the nave. He is a small man in red robes,
and has the clear eyes and skin of a child, and a
snow-white pointed beard. The waiting crowd turns
towards the chapel of the Sacrament, while the archbishop kneels for some minutes in adoration. Then
he proceeds to his throne in the choir. The mass is
now beginning; the young man is seated at the organ,
but to-day the Byzantine line of his plainsong is forgotten, and the choir revels in the light-hearted,
structureless emotion of nineteenth-century Italy. A
priest with a long ascetic face, dark against the white
walls of the church, eulogises Saint Catherine from
the pulpit in the choir. The music breaks out again;

incense and candle flames mix around the golden
retable as the office proceeds.· When at last, after the
quiet of its climax has been broken by the customary
three explosions, mass is over, the crowd surges around
the archbishop as he descends to the nave, eager to
kiss his ring. Now the square of the old city becomes
at last fully alive, as the people leaving the cathedral
wander round from booth to booth, choosing a place
at which to refresh themselves.

The festival with its procession that has just taken
place is one of a few that have survived, but formerly
stranger events took place on the grass where the
visitors are settling down to enjoy a meal. Here every
few years, the terrible procession of the Auto-da-fé
must have passed, the condemned clothed in shirts
painted with their effigies amid demons and flames,
often accompanied by the effigies and bones of those
who had died in prison and who thus were executed
post-mortem. Across this square, no doubt those in-
trepid missionaries set out for Tsaparang, a Tibetan
kingdom that they almost converted to Christianity;
and later, another explorer and missionary, Desideri,[20]
who was the first European to reach Leh, the capital
of the western Tibetan kingdom.

To-day, as the sun rises higher in the sky, the crowd
leaves as rapidly as it arrived; motor buses begin to

depart for the New City of Panjim. The road runs across a long stretch of salt marsh on a causeway, and finally enters the town over a bridge that spans a muddy creek of salt water. On the banks of this creek, jumping fish hop around on the drying mud, leaping by means of their fins which they have not learned to move alternately as the legs of a truly terrestrial beast are moved. In the heat of the day, as if propelled by the sun itself, water striders shoot about like balls of quicksilver on the surface of the water; later, in the cool evening, when the human inhabitants of the town come out again, the precarious progress of these insects on the boundary of sea and air will be so slow that they will seem like clockwork toys whose machinery wound up by the sun has now almost run down.

During the afternoon, the park in the central square of the New Town is not quite deserted, for several workmen are festooning electric lights around the bandstand. When they are in place, they are painted, some red and some green, and some are left unpainted; so that, if all goes well and the work can be completed before the band arrives, the national colours of Portugal will honour both Saint Catherine and the Republic alike. Part of the festoon cannot be painted in place and has to be taken down again. Men hurry away to get more paint. The current is turned on and off several times; the men who went to fetch more paint return with a large can. Finally, as the sun descends and a priest, in a cassock over striped cotton pyjamas, looks over the town from the top of the white steps that lead to the parish church of Panjim, the arrangements are complete. Soon the band begins to play. A crowd collects in the park and the people walk up and down, talking while they half listen. A few girls walk together, but the crowd is mostly made up of young men; one, a heavily built ruffian showing off his square black beard, was conspicuous among the recruits at the inspection in the morning outside the cathedral.

The sky suddenly turns pink with flecks of blue that darken and fuse toward the east. The trees flatten like shadows against this painted canvas sky. The band plays gaily; the crowd seems to walk faster. The girls have all come to one end of the path and, like a chorus, have grouped themselves together. In these few minutes after sunset, the square becomes so theatrical that it seems inevitable that all these people should start to sing, transforming the canvas sky into the backdrop of a musical romance, in which the principal lovers are to emerge shortly from behind the flat dark trees. But the night is unkind, enveloping the town so quickly that the whole lighting system of the stage is upset; the potential singers are forced to disperse and find their way home in the dark as best they can. The bandsmen put away their instru-ments; the operetta has finished, with the overture, just as the curtain went up.

Early the next morning, a false dawn awakens the country. Black clouds bank up on the horizon, ob-scuring its tender orange tint, and, when the sun renews its efforts half an hour later, it appears to the passengers on the little boat leaving the Island of Goa, in cruel, naked and barbaric splendour.

II

PAINTINGS ON A FAN

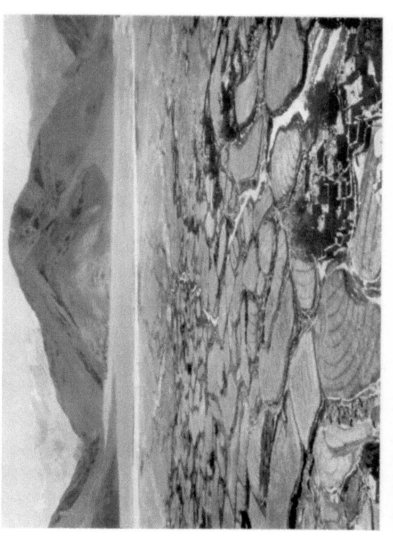

Plate VIII. Cultivated fan, and two desert fans in the distance, in the Upper Indus valley (from the gonpa on a rock above the village of Nyoma, Ladak).

PAINTINGS ON A FAN

THROUGHOUT the whole country of the Upper Indus, tributary streams come down from
snowy mountains into desert valleys. The detritus carried by these streams, and by the glaciers that
were there before them, has been deposited in the form
of fan-shaped plains, their wide ends cut by the main
river, their narrow ends pointing up to the mountains.
The surface of each expanse is streaked with the small
channels of the stream which has formed it, as if by
the lines of folds along which the fan could be closed.
In the uninhabited regions, this landscape is coloured
with many stony colours, brown, pale grey and dull
white, red and olive green. But, where there is enough
water for a village, the stream of the fan is artificially
led out in innumerable channels, and the living greens
of apricots, willow trees and little fields of barley make
the surrounding desert appear uniformly parched and
brown. Sometimes the water of the tributary is in-
sufficient to reach the lower part of a fan after the
upper regions have been irrigated; the green patch of
cultivation that surrounds a village then seems from
a distance to be receding into the mountains.

The settlements usually lie near a small spur of a

mountain, or a rocky hill may stand up in the middle
of the fan itself. In former days many of these spurs
and hills were fortified; they are favourite places for
religious houses, and many of the largest lamaist
monasteries or gonpas stand upon them. On these
fans, green at their narrow ends, then brown, and
perhaps fringed with more green where they touch the
main river, the life of Ladak[1] is painted; villages
cluster round the white gonpa on a fantastic rocky
knob, and across these fans the continual slow moving
backwards and forwards that characterises the life of
Central Asia takes place.

Along the edge of a very stony and immense fan,
pale grey-brown, a flock of some hundreds of dirty
sheep is moving westward, flowing in inconsequent
streamlets around the legs of three men in worn grey-
brown robes. Each beast bears on its back a double
bag of wool, carrying thirty pounds of Tibetan salt
toward India. The flock breaks a little; a small group
turns and mills round for a few minutes bleating.
Then what seemed to be an inconsequent streaming
round the caravan men, becomes a movement con-
sciously directed by them. From the road high up on
the other side of the river, the flock seems a small
moving fragment of the brown landscape; it has
momentarily broken, and now re-establishes its purpose

and its direction. The salt is carried on a little further. Some hours later, another flock of sheep carrying salt passes over the same stony pale grey-brown fan.

Fifty miles away a man rides alone, moving east up the Indus valley until he turns to the north to cross seven high passes. His grey robe is short, and on his feet he wears high leather boots; at his back, his possessions are fastened to his saddle, and above them is a monkey in a cage. A pilgrim returning from Mecca, he has bought a monkey in India to sell, perhaps to some Chinese official in Turkestan.

Between the great caravans of sheep and the willow garden where the Turki traveller has been resting, the little city of Leh is set on an irregular plain, whose edge the Indus has decorated with trees, swamps and cultivated land. A palace rises on a knob of rock against the mountains; another knob of rock by the river six miles away carries the white and red monastic building of Spithug; between them, brown-white sand and stones burn in an afternoon sun. The road that crosses the sand from the fields and water at Spithug to the fields and water at Leh is perhaps more frequented than any other in this region, but on many afternoons it is deserted. A few lizards run from rock to rock, dark desert beetles have taken refuge in the cooler sand below the larger stones.

Three figures come on to the fan from the west and, turning north, pass by the broken chorten at the base of the monastery at Spithug. A lady is riding ahead and behind her are a man and a woman attendant. The lady wears a dark plum-coloured dress, slit up in front to the waist over six feet of wrinkled trousers. Between two wings of false black hair, her head carries row upon row of turquoises sewn on to a wide strip of red. The rows of turquoise cascade down her back and are bordered on the left by a wide band of corals. Over the highest part of this headdress she has fastened a red hood, and has covered the lower part of the turquoise cascade with a Kashmir shawl of golden tawny yellow, strewn with flowers. Between the red hood and the bright folds of the shawl, the bands of blue stones glitter like a lake in a desert of coloured mountains. As she comes near and passes, she draws the hood over her face, for she is clearly a lady of rank and does not wish to be seen uncovered by strangers, but this does not prevent her turning to survey, from behind a fold of the hood, the only other traveller on the track. She pulls up her horse for an instant and then trots on over several miles of sandy road toward the barley fields of Leh, disappearing on the east side of the town that lies below the deserted palace.

Turquoises are universally worn by these Buddhist people, by men as well as women. The poorer men may have but a single ear-ring, a simple circle of silver wire bearing a pair of blue beads, with a red bead between them; these, though often of glass, are in-tended to appear as turquoise and coral. The more affluent peasants wear necklaces of turquoise and coral, onyx and amber beads. Every Buddhist woman, however poor, wears a berag² or headdress, on which turquoises are set. Some may have but a single row of poor greenish stones, and even in such a short row there may be gaps from which stones have been lost. A woman as wealthy as the lady who has just ridden up to the fan carries a huge blue waterfall in mosaic, covering her head and descending to the middle of her back. In the territory around Leh, the front of such a large berag always bears a single very fine stone called *dun-yu*; behind this is another single stone, the succeeding pieces being smaller and set in rows. On the crown of the head are two amulet cases of gold and silver; behind them the blue pavement is interrupted by a row of cornelians. Only the wealthiest of ladies wear rows of coral beads on the left side of their berags.

Nearly every woman carries pinned to her dress, over the left breast, a silver brooch ornamented with

turquoise beads, from which hang tweezers, a tooth-
pick, spatulas for cleaning the ears, and such-like
implements. Side by side with the silver and the blue-
green stones of these marine-coloured adornments, she
wears seashells from the Indian Ocean; they are an
essential part of the most interesting article of her complex attire. This ornament, the Tibetan name of which
is *ldo-cha*, consists of a large perforated plaque of brass,
cast in the form of a fret and supposed to represent
the entrails of Gautama Buddha's mother. It is worn
on the right hip, from which Gautama is supposed
to have issued miraculously. Below the brass fret, a
needlecase is fixed and from this needlecase six long
chains of cowries hang, the end of each chain bearing
a little bell. The whole of this elaborate and universally
worn ornament clearly originated as a charm to pro-
mote female fertility. The brass plaque, representing
the loins from which Shakya-muni sprang, itself suggests this meaning. The festoons of cowries, called
rum-bu, a name apparently implying the womb,
scarcely admit of any other interpretation. Cowry
shells are well-known symbols of the female sexual
organs; with small figures emerging from their aper-
tures, they are frequently introduced into paintings of
the daemonic forms of gods with their female energies
or saktis. Strings of cowries may be worn in addition

to those on the *ldo-cha*; the beautiful brown speckled shells of giant species are often strung singly by such women as can obtain them. The needlecase from which the ropes of shells hang may appear to be a purely utilitarian object, but, however practically useful they may seem, needles also have a magical potency. They are sometimes fastened in the hats of children, where they probably perform the same anti-daemonical func-tions as are ascribed to the spears and tridents placed on the roofs of Tibetan houses. Needles are also regarded as suitable offerings for the altars of the gods.

The Mohammedan women, for the most part ugly and careworn, who inhabit the country around Dras to the south-west of Leh, relieve the drabness of their dark formless dresses with an ornament not unlike the *ldo-cha*. The people of this region were once Buddhists; sculptured monoliths on which Boddhisattvas and a stupa are represented, still stand outside the village of Dras; some pieces of carved stone by the roadside may indicate the site of a temple. The ornament worn by the women of Dras therefore may have had a common origin with that worn by the Buddhist women further east. But the plaque is now replaced by a smaller circle of brass with a single horizontal crossbar, from which hang beads, usually white or blue; sometimes there are a few red ones. In the place of the needlecase, the ornament may be provided with a small amulet case, probably containing texts from the Koran. This vestigial form of *ldo-cha* may be fastened on either side of the woman's gown; frequently two are worn, one on each side, and a second smaller pair may ornament the shoulders. The white beads appear to replace the cowries festooned at the side of the freer and more comely Buddhist women. The blue and red beads suggest that once coral and turquoise may also have had a part in the lifegiving design.

Most of the substances used in the making of the proud and heavy display of jewellery that the Ladakis wear, must be brought into the country from outside. A little gold was once obtained locally, but coral and amber, cowries and turquoises, must always have been imported into Indian Tibet. The coral and cowries are brought from the sea coast; the turquoises appear to come in part from Persia, in part from the far eastern parts of Tibet. Barley and wool, goat's meat, butter, apricots and a few vegetables, enough wood to build the framework of a house of air-dried brick, nearly all the staple requirements of life can be obtained from the cultivated patches on the fans and in the more sheltered mountain valleys. Enough tea must be brought into the country to supply its needs, for everyone drinks tea mixed with flour, and with butter when there is butter to spare. Salt and soda, added as a seasoning to this buttered tea, come from the margins of the salt and alkaline lakes of the Tibetan plateau far to the east. Implements of iron and steel, utensils of copper and brass, are also imported. Every man carries a steel blade, to which is attached a pouch containing tinder and a flake of flint for making a fire. The form of the flint, flat and square with bevelled edges, suggests that it has come from England. At Brandon in Suffolk, one or two men still knap flint flakes of this very pattern; they suppose that the flints are sent to China for use in flint-lock guns. But, among all these articles of commerce, the substances traditionally used as ornaments bulk large in both quantity and value. Lumps of turquoise heaped in little piles may be seen in the upper room of a mer-chant's house in Leh; another merchant, trading chiefly with Lhasa, deals in silk and turquoises, arnica and tea. The trade in traditionally precious and ornamental substances must have played no small part in keeping open the brigand-infested roads of the Tibetan plateau, and in establishing the routes which run toward India over the brown and stony fans, facili-tating the journeys of pilgrims and lamas, and the inter-change of tradition and learning, binding the Tibetan-speaking peoples into a uniform spiritual whole.[3]

Early in the year, while the barley was being sown, a small procession might have been seen travelling on the road from Leh toward Kashmir, travelling till now it has reached the limits of the Buddhist country. Drums are heard in a monastery that stands on the far bank of a stream flowing between tilled and still unsown barley fields. Outside the monastery, horses are waiting. In the distance, figures appear from the building; they cross a garden to perform some cere, mony before a group of three chortens, red, white and blue. Then the sound of instruments grows louder, as the people in the distance mount their horses and ride across the ford. A great lama from Lhasa, the Ngaris Skushok, has come to bless the fields and receive gifts from the people. His retinue moves across the fans from place to place, from gonpa to gonpa. A soldier in red with a Chinese straw hat tied on with red ribbon, bearing an old Russian rifle painted red, leads the procession on a prancing white horse. Then rides an attendant in a flowered grey and dark blue robe. Behind him, two men walk playing drums and horns, while a third carries a pole ornamented at the top with a bundle of prayer flags and feathers. Next rides the Skushok himself, a middle-aged man with a shrewd Chinese face, wearing a plum-coloured robe and a yellow clerical hat. Behind him come two elderly figures, also dressed in the plum-coloured robes of lamas, and seemingly both men, but actually the father and mother of the great ecclesiastic. One of them, apparently the father, carries a brown pug dog, whose head emerges from his dull red robe, and behind him, bringing up the procession, rides another lama with a black and white pug. Villagers, bringing incense of smouldering wood on plates, come up as the procession passes through their fields. The Skushok initiates the sowing, throwing grain on either side of him, travelling through the land to make it fruitful.

The Skushok has left the fans of the Indus valley; he has passed through the fantastic valley of Lamayuru and below the ruined rock fort of Bod Kharbu. To-day he is blessing the fields just above Mulbe. Here on a large rock, a huge figure of Cham-pa, carved in relief in the tenth century, looks down on the road. A little chapel has been built for his feet, and, from the roof of this, poles bound round with flowers have been placed, leaning against the statue. From a crag, two little monasteries look down on to the village; below lie four miles of valley still unsown. The road then turns sharply to the right and leaves the Buddhist country at Shargola, where the last tiny gonpa hangs precariously on a cliff of glacial gravel, like a white moth clinging to a wall.

At Lamayuru, the barley seed is already sprouting. The village lies near the top of a valley filled with the fine deposit of an interglacial lake. This has been eroded into great blocks and tiny pinnacles, below which, wherever there is level ground and a supply of water, fields have been tilled and planted. On the largest block, its pale surface pitted with smoke-stained caves from which the entrances have long fallen away, stands a large gonpa. The place was once a sanctuary of the Bon religion, a faith that grew side by side with Buddhism from the primitive beliefs of the Tibetans, till now, surviving in parts of eastern Tibet, it seems to have become merely a form of Lamaism from which little save Shakya-muni is omitted. Only a few paintings discovered in a broken temple doubtfully remain from the old religion,[4] but in those days the sanctuary was known as Yung-drung, from a patch of sacrificial grain which sprouted miraculously in the form of a swastika.

To-day, as the barley begins to germinate, a dozen or so women are working in the afternoon sun, carrying stone from an informal roadside quarry; several lamas and an old *jo-mo* supervise the work. Later in the day a large party is given in the gonpa. Two rows of men sit back to back on the ground down the middle of an oblong court. At one end of the court is a raised verandah, poorly painted with figures of deities, on which the lamas of the gonpa are seated. A small group of women, dressed in the worn red costume of *jo-mos*,[5] sit on the floor of the court, below one end of the verandah. At the other end, in a raised recess, an important lama sits with a young man in a red robe and a red gold-ribbed skull cap. In the far corner of the court, below the monastic buildings, a number of women are seated huddled together. Opposite the dais are two musicians, one playing a pair of drums, the other a wooden pipe. In front of them, four men and a boy are dancing. Each wears an ordinary robe of coarsely woven wool and has a scarf of the same stuff. They dance in a line, holding out the ends of their scarves on a level with their shoulders, facing the audience, turning, following the leader in a sinuous line, retreating, turning again. The dance stops; a man comes round with barley wine, called *chang*. Everyone carries a wooden bowl lined with silver, and holds these to be filled from a pitcher of brass and silver. Several more women come in to join the party; as they pass opposite the frescoed verandah, they prostrate themselves three times, holding their hands in prayer in front of their faces and their breasts before each prostration. But, though they bow their faces to the ground, they take care to keep the fine stones on the front of their berags from being pressed into the dirt. At the side of the verandah, the young man in the gold-ribbed red skull cap drinks a great deal of *chang*. The dancing begins again; the line of men re-forms, and some of the women who have just arrived form a second similar line. They dance the same steps as the men, but accompany the movements with formal opening and turning of the hands, which are free to posture in this way as they do not hold scarves. The young man in the red skull cap comes out into the court to lead the men's line. He starts a little unsteadily, developing a very elegant, dignified and affected style, but his movements unfortunately are too sporadic to fit with the established pattern of the dance, so that, although he has assumed the position of its leader, he soon becomes detached from it, gyrating about to his own great satisfaction, like the severed head of some gay insect that might wave its jaws and antennae, leaving the trunk to continue reflexly its own activities. Several times the music stops and while the dancers pause, *chang* is again brought round, the young red-capped man filling his bowl more frequently than the others. At last they weary of dancing; all the dancers retire to a low building at the back of the court. A few women come from their corner and join the double row of men; all continue drinking and talking as the sun slips behind the mountains.

At the back of the neglected drums of the now silent musicians, the monastic buildings stand in an irregular pile. Along a wall, a row of prayer wheels is flipped by a passing lama who is walking down a pathway on the top of a low roof. The buildings might be blocks of the soft filling of the valley, the chortens that stand around them, strangely weathered pinnacles. A little below the main buildings, a small temple stands by itself. At the back, a figure of Chen-re-zi with a thousand arms, the palm of each hand bearing an eye, looks serenely into the darkening chapel, from below his cone of nineteen additional faces. Four large arms, isolated from the rest, are draped with cobwebby white material. The image stands in a chamber cut off from the chapel, and is seen through a crude wooden grille. One side of the hall is painted with daemonic forms of gods, each embracing his female energy or sakti, without which he would be powerless to grant the requests of the kneeling suppliants, whose prayers rise as white lines to the divine and grotesque faces of the gods. The rest of the walls is divided into irregular rectangles by dull red lines. In each panel are painted scenes of the life of Buddha. There is no element of design in the placing of these on the walls, but each scene in itself is an exquisite arrangement of figures on a subdued green land. The country is so green that the sky is green there, fading to a paler green on the horizon, the background deepening again where the green earth runs out to meet the sky. Against this quiet landscape are set little figures, groups of listening disciples, processions, kings on horses, drawn in a calligraphic Chinese manner, gaily coloured in white, yellow, orange and red, the very colours of the rocks which make up the inani⁄mate part of the landscape outside.

In another chapel of the main building, painted in the present century, the tradition is entirely different. All the walls of this large upper room have been included in a single array of gods and saints. Chinese influence[6] is apparent in the drawing, but this in⁄fluence is continually struggling with Indian postures and Saivatic attributes. Such a struggle is very charac⁄teristic of Tibetan painting. The daemonic gods, embracing their saktis in the yab⁄yum attitude, fes⁄tooned with strings of skulls, carrying thunderbolts and rosaries of cowries from which tiny figures are emerging, recall in the slightly varying positions of their innumerable arms and legs, the dynamic decom⁄position of the Italian futurists. But they have resisted all those quieter forces of the most distant East that

Plate IX. The Guru Padma-sambhava, Lamayuru Gonpa, twentieth century.

have crystallised in gentle saints, meditating among rocks below pagoda-capped mountains, on adjacent parts of the wall.

These paintings in the upper chapel at Lamayuru show what a modern Tibetan artist can achieve. The walls are covered with figures and floral scroll work, but tend to be broken into sections by the use of the same predominant colour in adjacent figures. A group of saints, with hands depicted in varying stylised ritual attitudes, colours half the wall opposite the door with flaming red, which breaks against a dark blue dae-monic god embracing a pinkish sakti. To the right, a fierce-eyed Padma-sambhava, floating between smaller celestial copulations, introduces the red again in his voluminous robe. The chapel contains but a single small gilded chorten, and has several large windows, so that the walls are unusually well lighted and easily seen. This gives the decorative skill of the artist a rare opportunity to display itself, and he has made every use of it; but, however endlessly his highly finished scroll work carries the eye through crowded supernatural territories, the more ambitious scheme lacks the quiet beauty of the older painting in the little temple below.

A third temple room is unpainted; one side is stacked with the hundred and eight volumes of the lamaistic canon or Kan-chur; the other walls are bare. But the whole room is crowded with painted flags and images, trays of offerings of grain, paper flowers, and festoons of the flat diaphanous seed vessels of some exotic plant. In an important gonpa, the chapels become filled with such accumulations of sacred bric-à-brac. At Basgo, a temple room which contains an immense and very ancient figure of Cham-pa is lighted only from an upper gallery, which gives access to the head of the image. On entering from the bright light outside, the room seems like a tropical forest at night. The boughs of the trees of the jungle gradually resolve themselves into the arms of the image and the pillars of the temple; what seems to be moonlight streaming through branches, becomes the sun playing on the colossal head and shoulders of the Buddha-to-come. A mass of lianes and epiphytes resolves itself into streamers and painted temple flags, among which a host of squat and fearsome beasts become little gods, piled up among offerings of barley, cowry shells, coins, sewing needles, and a piece of the much valued bitumen which, emerging from a crack in a cliff near Kalatze, may be shot down in small pieces, worth their weight in silver, by a good marksman.

But, if the chapel where Cham-pa sits at Basgo is quasi-tropical in its darkness, a more truly tropical

and brilliant light fills the little temple called Sum-
tzag, which is part of a gonpa in the ancient village
of Alchi. Alchi lies at the edge of an irregular fan
on the south side of the Indus. The gonpa is hidden
in apricot trees; the path into it passes through arched
chortens. The chapel itself is white with a very simple
two-storeyed portico of carved wooden pillars. Such
carved pillars are only found in the oldest gonpas
built by Kashmiri monks. A large tree trunk cut
with notches gives access to an upper storey of the
verandah, and from this a door leads into the gallery
of the temple. Three large statues stand in niches;
their bodies are to be venerated from below, their
heads from the gallery. In the middle of the temple
stands a silvery chorten, and in its honour a tattered
yellow canopy hangs from the middle of the lantern-
like roof. Looking down from the gallery, illumined
by the sun which streams through the open door, the
silvery chorten seems at first to rise up from an indefinite pit, which is relieved only by two tiny flames
that flicker on butter lamps left by worshippers. As
the darkness becomes less intense, the plastered walls
between the niches in which stand the great images
turn into a pattern of coloured squares on a blue,
printed fabric. Finally, in each blue square a little
Buddha is seen, seated within a halo of dull red. But,

as the eye turns upwards again to the walls of the gallery, the ultramarine of the background has become so rich in the sunlight that it shines like gold around the figures painted on it. The chapel is filled with a jewelled splendour only equalled by the mosaic-lined churches of the Byzantines.

To the left, above the niche from which the head of an immense Bhodhisattva peeps out over the gallery floor, Chen-re-zi stands white against a flowered ground. On either side of him are two maidens in attendance. Their breasts have swollen to overflowing above the neckline of their short-sleeved jackets, while their hips, like waterfalls, seem to have carried their skirts down to the very brink of a cascade, where they maintain a precarious hold on the widest part of the maidens' bodies, waiting to be carried away in a moment by the descending rush of the stream. But, with all this fullness, as of fruit ripening after tropical rain, the painter has kept the geometrical properties of a perfectly flat pattern always in his mind. The line is calligraphic, but, in the arrangement of the drapery, each area demarcated by folds has so rich a texture, that the figures are built up of an abstract pattern of areas of different colours and qualities of surface, rather than of the conventionally linear pen strokes of an oriental brush.

66

Plate X. Detail of mural in the upper gallery of the Sum-tzag temple at Alchi; sixteenth century, based on an earlier painting.

Opposite Chen-re-zi, a greyish yellow figure of
Dol-ma stands as saviouress to a number of little men
caught as the victims of various calamities; some flee
from snakes, others from stampeding elephants, or the
wrath of man. In the miniaturist treatment of these
men and animals, no less than in the tropical abundance of the maidens on the opposite wall, the painter
betrays his Indian origin. Opposite the door a golden
Shakya-muni is seated, and below him are scenes of
instruction, but the disciples have left the green land
of Lamayuru gonpa and have wandered into other
coloured countries, so that they meditate and listen,
now against a red, now a yellow landscape. Between
the main figures over the niches, the walls are filled
with mandalas, curious designs containing nine deities,
arranged in a square within a circle; between the
mandalas, every space is occupied by a seated god or
goddess. More of the magic squares fill the walls of
the little lantern in the roof. Only over the door is any
god represented in a daemonic form; here a six-armed
figure in dark blue seems to keep guard over the innumerable little gods and goddesses on the walls.
Some of these small seated figures show the most perfect work in the whole chamber. Not all are uniformly excellent; many on the south wall appear to
be hurriedly executed, and are perhaps the work of

an apprentice. But, in a little white goddess on the north wall, low down on the right hand of the figure of Chen-re-zi, all the art of the larger figures has been concentrated and crystallised. Though her head and body are borne on so thin a waist, that she seems like a sea star or hydroid whose thin stem would collapse but for the support of the circumambient water, and though the base that her hips afford seems solid enough, yet again both this delicacy and this solidity are achieved only by the inflections of a calligraphic line, set over intricately patterned areas of drapery.

But when at last admiration gives place to curiosity, which turning aside from the direct appeal of these walls to the eye, and from the mythology that they were made to represent, and from that more insistent mythology that enters the mind of every observer of the half-known, enquires who painted these walls, the answer, as far as can be told, is a strange one. Two records throw some light on the question. From a Tibetan history it appears that Kashmiri monks, who between A.D. 996 and 1000 founded several such monasteries, finally built a gonpa at Alchi because they had paint left over from the building of the others. An inscription in the temple itself, however, seems to indicate that all the present painting in the Sum-tzag temple is of considerably later date, for on the

base of one of the statues in the building is a statement
of the amount of red, blue and gold paint contributed
by the local peasantry, when the temple was restored
by King Tashi-namgyal.[7] The paintings in their present state all seem to be contemporary, so that the
entire decoration of the temple must have been done
at this time, probably by an Indian painter who
adhered as far as possible to the ancient design on the
walls. That much of the ancient design has been preserved is undoubtedly indicated by the colouring of
the background in blue and dull red, which would
seem to ally the work to the very ancient Buddhist art
of Turkestan. But so many of the details, the little
men and animals around Dol-ma, the dresses of the
attendants, and particularly the curious full-faced eyes
of the seated profile figures, may so fairly be attributed
to the later painter, that it is justifiable to credit him
with having produced the beauty of the whole, and to
suppose that an artist, probably a Gujerati, had found
his way to the court of King Tashi-namgyal, and there
absorbed as much of the ancient Buddhist art as he
needed to cover it in a fuller and more developed style.
So that he has left in this little temple on the Indus
amid the apricot trees, barley fields and burnt brown
rocks below the snow, one of the works of Indian art
most directly comprehensible to modern Western eyes.

Now the barley has sprouted up around each village; the sun mounts higher in the sky each noon.
Though sheep and yaks have to be driven to further
pastures, and water supplied to each farm in turn
from the channels on the fans, the pressure of work is
less than at the time of the sowing. Little groups sit
about outside houses in the villages, spinning, turning
copper prayer mills, talking. The moon wanes and a
new moon approaches; before the next new moon the
sun will already be declining. Fresh travellers appear
on the fans, and their movements are more directed
than before, for in the first few days of June a thousand
or more people are journeying to Hemis Gonpa. The
Skushok of this monastery is the chief Guru of Ladak;
the people are going to his monastery to receive his
blessing and to see the dances that are held there at
this time.

East of the broken fan which carries the palace of
Leh near its base, and Spithug Gonpa on its margin,
the Indus, whose course for the most part is in a
narrow barren valley interrupted by stony fans wherever a tributary joins the stream, has flowed for a brief
twenty miles along a fault line. Cutting into the softer,
newer rocks on the south, the river in its repeated
wanderings has levelled a wide fertile plain. Large
fans still run down to meet the river, but they end

abruptly against swampy fields, so that a man can stand with one foot in a desert and the other on damp green grass. All around this part of the valley lie the principal villages of the country. For most of the pilgrims, from the west of Leh and from the city itself, the road leads through these swampy fields. On a fan to the south stands the little palace of Stag. The Gyalpo and his queen, with their son and two daughters, have already left for the monastery. Opposite, on the north side of the valley at Sheh, stands another palace, a large horizontal block capped by an immense chorten. Further upstream, a rock towers above the barley fields at Tigtse and carries on its summit an immense monastic building, whose receding lines continue the converging contours of the rock on which it stands. The eastern face of the rock is covered with a maze of little houses for lamas. At the summit, in front of the largest chapel, a young lama is cleaning large brass and copper jugs and like ceremonial vessels. Above him in a gallery apartment sits another and very aged lama; the hairs of his scanty beard seem to repeat vertically the horizontal iron wires of his spectacles. He squats cross-legged, fumbling with his rosary, a tea cup at his side.

Bright clear light pours through the door of the large chapel. Its walls are painted richly and competently, but somewhat conventionally. On the right, the golden-faced Shakya-muni almost smiles at a goddess on the opposite side of the temple, around whom yellow-capped saints are meditating. There is a seated statue of Tsong-ka-pa in front of the western wall, and some glass-doored cabinets contain the more daemonic gods. The whole hall is bright when the light fills it, bright and elaborate with the elaborateness of second-childhood, appropriate to the old lama in the gallery, who is fumbling with his beads and drinking his tea, surrounded by the flags of the goddess Dol-ma and photographs of the Tashi Lama and other incarnate deities of Tibet. A cloud now obscures the sun and a small wind whistles ominously around the upper part of the rock on which the gonpa stands. Two small doorways in the western wall of the temple lead to another chamber, a shallow gallery lighted by two small windows. In this furthest recess stands a single image of Shakya-muni, unperturbed by his followers and interpreters, and by the pantheon they have imagined. The walls around him are not peopled with gaily coloured saints, but covered with a wash of a light and cold grey. Against this background, hung head downward like carcases in a butcher's shop, the bodies of men and animals are painted in white, greys, pinks and dull reds. These carcases, hanging

Plate XI. Detail of mural in Tigtse Gonpa; probably seventeenth to eighteenth century.

from a geometrical frieze, are opened, scalped and eviscerated in every way, so that they resemble copies of anatomical charts. Kidneys, brains, hearts, lungs burst out from them. Below parade two rows of animals, superbly drawn in black on the grey wall, horses, yaks, tigers, vultures, some of them reaching for the viscera of the anatomised beings that swing above them. A small plant is growing in a china pot on the sill of one of the windows; the wind whistles ominously through the other. Above the rock to the north the desert mountains rise to meet the snow; below the rock lie the barley fields. Between them, this grey chamber seems to float in the wind, and in it sits Gautama, imprisoned by two doors too small to allow him to escape from the horrors depicted on its walls.

When, above Stag and Sheh, above the rock on which Tigtse gonpa stands and the rock on which the royal monastery of Stag-sna was built by Ngag-bang-nam-gyal, above the fan that bears in the distance a gonpa where two lamas become possessed and pro-phesy, the valley finally narrows, the fields completely disappear. Only a thistle every fifty feet or so suggests that water has made the channel and the fans. Far in front the turquoises on the head of a lady dance in the sun over a red and green cloak, as she ambles along on her pony. The road passes over four miles of desert; then, as the valley again widens a little and a village appears near the river, two long mani walls run down from the top of a fan and seem to deflect travellers into the mountains to the south, as waves are deflected by a breakwater. Caravans and single tra-vellers have been diverted by those walls since the earliest morning light. Now, as the sun rises high enough to illuminate fully its splendour, a procession is moving over the fan, slowly creeping along the left side of the western mani wall toward the poplar trees in the Hemis valley. Once inside this ravine, the way leads past innumerable chortens and lha-thos gro-tesquely ornamented with daemonic faces. Further up, the water of the stream in the valley is led out to irrigate terraces. The road turns, runs along the base of a slope planted with poplars, and dips to a little bridge over the stream. Above the bridge rises the large rambling building of Hemis Gonpa. From the poplars a low growl is heard; two lamas are playing eight-foot trumpets, the ends of which are supported on the shoulders of a boy. They pass the melody, such as it is, from one to the other, so that each has ample time to regain breath. The procession passes and descends to the little bridge. Lamas with peaked hats walk ahead, holding drums on poles which they beat with a long lever. Behind them are others playing pipes. A lama in a red feathered hat follows the musicians and with him is a man whose face is shielded by a five-pointed crown of flat pieces of wood inverted over his forehead. Finally comes the Skushok of Pheang, the visiting ecclesiastic in whose honour the trumpets have again just been sounded, for now the trumpeters have walked rapidly round to another point of vantage. The Skushok rides on a brown horse; he wears a lemon-yellow robe, with a dull red scarf over his right shoulder, and on his head a flat-brimmed hat, with a central knob of gilt lacquer. As the trumpeters blow their second salute, a large parasol is brought out of the monastery and held over the Skushok as he rides up to the monastery gate, while a great crowd, mostly of women, stands watching with hands held together in prayer.

At four in the afternoon, the lamas of the monastery assemble in one of the largest chapels. Much of the floor of the chapel is covered with cakes of meal modelled into chortens and set out in rows. At the back of the hall a great number of small cup-like lamps,[8] filled with melted butter, twinkle in the half-darkness like crocuses in a March evening. Their light spreads around a large central altar decorated with un-natural paper flowers. In front the lamas sit, reading in a low mumbling voice from service books. On either side, before the altar, the Skushok of Hemis and the aged titulary king of Ladak are seated on low thrones which raise them a little above the others; they are refreshed with tea from time to time. Services continue through-out the evening and during the succeeding day. At night, by the light of stars and of camp fires, the gonpa is vaguely visible against the hill; when the great trumpets sound, it seems like a huge ship ready to sail off from its moorings on the mountain and travel up the Indus into the furthest recess of Tibet. About three in the morning a few pilgrims stir round the main gate; a narrow crack between the doors of one of the larger chapels collects light from myriads of butter lamps. The trumpets sound, alternating with a sweet melody played on shawms, which dies and rises again. Then more people stir and a lama comes into the court with a kerosene lamp. By six an im-mense flag of Padma-sambhava has been hung on the wall of the courtyard, and before it stands a tem-porary altar. The flag is considered very sacred and is exhibited at the dances every twelfth year. During the next few hours, pilgrims go in a continuous stream past the flag, bowing their heads so as to touch its lower edge with their foreheads. Mothers lift their babies and bring their reluctant little heads in contact

with the bright silk border of the banner. This adoration continues for two or three hours, as pilgrims
arrive to take their places in the court.

The theme of the performance that they are awaiting
is usually supposed to be the fate of the soul of the
heretic king Lang-dar-ma, who was the most vigorous
opponent of Tibetan Buddhism in the early middle
ages. He was murdered in A.D. 900 by a monk, who
became filled with pity for the king who was accumu-
lating sins by his persecution of the lamas. "Mounted
on a white horse blackened with charcoal, and wearing
a roomy woollen cloak black on the outside and white
on the inside, he went to Lhasa. With him he took
an iron bow and an iron arrow. When he came to
Lhasa he saw The Strong One reading the inscription on Long Stone, with his back turned to the
Temple and the Cho-ten of Gan-den. He alighted
in The Strong One's presence. He bent the bow,
resting it on his knee. The king thought he was doing
obeisance to him. During the first obeisance he bent
the bow; during the second he fitted the arrow-notch
to the bow-string; during the third he let fly. The
arrow pierced the king's chest. He stayed to call out,
'I am the demon, Black Ya-she. When anybody
wishes to kill a sinful king, let him do it as I have
killed this one.' So saying, he fled. The cry was raised,

'The Strong One is killed in Lhasa, pursue the assassin.' But the monk washed the black off his horse in a pond, and turned his cloak inside out. And now he called out, 'I am the god called White Nam-te-u', and continued his flight."[9]

The stylisation of the story may be no more than that which generally marks the simplicity of such records, yet here history reads more as ceremonial than as actual occurrence. This thought perhaps should be dismissed from the mind, for in the dance that is beginning there is no definite trace of the ritual implied. The entire performance is indeed like a broken painted window, on which is depicted some event derived from an actual occurrence that is taking place outside. Fragments of the play are seen through holes half-stuffed with straw; a more perfect but quite conventionalised picture is painted on the glass itself, but this in its turn is partly obliterated by the fact that an entirely irrelevant drama is being played in front of the window.

Two thousand people are seated on the roofs round the courtyard, in galleries, on the floor of the courtyard itself. Most of the women have collected into a large group below a gallery; looking down on them, they seem a plum-coloured lake on which waves of black hair are breaking into surf of turquoise blue.

Plate XII. Group of women assembled for the Black Hat Dance at Hemis Gonpa.

Around this pool, the greyish robes of the men seem to melt into the earthen floor of the court, and among them the red or yellow caps of visiting lamas stand out like dusty flowers. Two youths with grotesque white masks keep clear the centre of the court with whips. They choose a pretty girl as their victim and beat her, as she screams with laughter, into the laps of her friends behind. Other girls come with pitchers, from which they sprinkle water over the dusty floor of the court, for a light breeze has risen.

There is a low throne in a recess in the wall of the courtyard, opposite the door of the large chapel in which the performers are now preparing themselves. In front of this throne, a small papier-mâché altar has been set; on it are incense sticks, piles of rose petals, and bowls. Lamas are preparing the altar and throne for the Skushok; a dorje, or symbol of a thunderbolt, and a bell are brought out from the chapel and placed on the altar. A man in a black robe lined with red, white trousers, a gold and black hat, a cerise scarf, blue tassel on his pigtail, and dark horn-rimmed sunglasses, fusses round, adjusting a carpet and inspecting the preparations.

The Skushok of Hemis enters the courtyard, wearing the ordinary red robe of a lama, and is preceded by musicians who always walk before him when he goes about the monastery on ceremonial duties. He is a short, middle-aged man, with a kind and intelligent face. When he arrives at his throne, he is vested in magnificent robes of white Chinese silk, on which an intricate and many-coloured pattern is embroidered. On his head he now wears a high pink silk hat, wider at the crown than at the brim. A bowl of yellow liquid is brought to the lamas around the Skushok's throne, and from it offerings are flicked into the air.

The performance begins with a dance by a group of lamas, dressed in robes of Chinese silk. They wear broad-brimmed black hats, which bear on their crowns either the image of a skull or a sacred monogram. Their faces are painted with soot, a spot on each cheek, a line down the nose, just as newly born babies are painted, to make them unrecognisable as human children when the demons crowd round to attack them. Each lama carries a spoon made in the form of a human skull cap and decorated with streamers. They dance round the court in a ring, taking two steps forward and then turning on one leg. Though the steps are somewhat reminiscent of an English Morris dance, the passage of time, as in a slow-motion picture, has been greatly retarded by their padded woollen boots. They produce from their robes wisps of some dried plant and continue dancing, holding these in their hands. These dancers are generally supposed to represent the priests of the pre-lamaistic Bon religion; their hats, from which the name of the entire festival, the Black Hat Dance, is derived, bear Sivaitic skulls and the lamaistic mono-gram, so that much has been added to their ancient insignia. Lamas now bring two objects like models of eggs, one brown and one white, in egg cups, on a dish, also a fire pot and a vase of peacock feathers; they are carried out of sight toward the door and the end of this ritual cannot be seen. The dancers retire two by two up the steps of the chapel whence they came.

There is a long pause; the buffoons who have been keeping order entertain the crowd by mimicking Euro-pean visitors, so that the whips, which they have been using for threatening the front row, now become matches, a cigarette, or the handle of a cinematograph camera.

In new costumes, the sixteen dancers finally appear, again two by two. They have changed their hats for gilded masks with long vertical eye-slits, so that now they seem to be helmeted. After the dance of these helmeted performers, there is another long pause.

A procession appears from the chapel. First come two lamas with hats like cocks' combs, playing pipes, then two with large but empty censers, and another

with a jug. After them, come dancers with huge
masks representing the chief deities of lamaism, Dol-
ma, Gautama Buddha, and some of the terrible-
looking daemonic gods. Padma-sambhava, who
comes last, is larger than any of them and is honoured
with a canopy. After the gods come numerous attendants carrying various objects of ritual significance,
such as a conch shell, a magic mirror, and a staff
carved at the top with the face of a man; then sixteen
lamas with high pentagonal hats, and scarves over
their mouths. Behind these come two clowns, grotesque hairy old men. The gods arrange themselves in
a group, as if for a family photograph, with Padma-
sambhava under his canopy, and the attendants, with
their curious objects, standing around. The sixteen
lamas with covered mouths seat themselves in a row
on a long carpet. Then four masked dancers in green
enter to amuse the celestial gathering. They are replaced by four girlish figures, who continue the dance.
The clowns mock the dancers and jump around the
seated lamas. The entertainment is primarily in honour
of Padma-sambhava, and is concluded by each god
and goddess rising and performing a *pas-seul* before
the Guru under the canopy. This celebration, in
which Shakya-muni has to dance in honour of the
greatest traducer of his doctrine, concludes the morn-

82

ing's performance. There is a long interval until the ceremony begins again in the afternoon; and, during this the hottest and dustiest time of the day, it seems that much of the irrelevance of the performance in front of the imagined window has disappeared. Padma-sambhava, who saw the dances, has retired into the chapel and has removed his mask. Padma-sambhava on the huge banner has been replaced by the founder of the Druk-pa order of lamas, on a smaller banner over the altar in the court. But, when the dancing begins again, a new note of irrelevancy of an older time is introduced; a number of demons enter, followed by two men dressed like caricatures of apes, and there follows a dance by demons, whose high head-dresses are decorated with models of entrails, in red, white and blue, as the drums and cymbals begin to sound again after the noon-day pause.

The middle of the court becomes empty again; the Skushok is not present, even though the culmination of the ceremonial is approaching. Two lamas bring in a small board, on which lies a little image covered with an indigo-violet shroud. The stuff of the shroud is half-transparent; through it can be seen the outlines of a man's figure bound up, its legs bent as if trussed. In front of this figure, a small carpet is placed. A lama now comes and, standing on the carpet,

recites a long prayer. He holds a cup which is filled
from a pitcher by an attendant, then, adding a little
barley to the cup, he pours three libations around the
shrouded image. Four demons enter with chains, a
hook-like knife and a bell; they dance around the
image for a long time and retire. Four more dancers
come; their costumes are painted to look like the
bones of a skeleton. They do another square dance
around the image, and one of them seizes the shroud
and retires shrieking. The image is now disclosed as
a little figure of meal, with a tall pointed hat such as
saints wear when painted meditating in the desert.
Preceded by musicians and lamas carrying censers and
a jug, a figure enters the empty centre of the court,
wearing magnificent robes and a huge daemonic three-
eyed mask, coloured red. This demon begins a slow
dance around the court; his deliberate movements
accentuate the grotesqueness of the mask and add
terror to the dancer. He carries a large straight knife.
After dancing for a few minutes, a lama gives the
demon a little grain which he throws into the air.
Four more demons come down the steps of the chapel
into the court, and the dance is continued in a ring.
The first demon finally kneels on the carpet, and,
raising his knife over the image, chops it into little
bits. A piece is given to each of his attendants, and

they all retire, to be replaced by five other demons who are given fragments. The remains of the figure are moulded together and removed. This image then was the soul of the heretic king which, wearing a cap like a saint, is bound, receives sacrifice as a god, descends into hell perhaps, as the earth on which it lies is trampled by the dancing feet of daemonic torturers and deaths, and finally, cut to bits by the chief of the demons, is given to his followers as a ritual meal. But, as the court is again cleared, any meaning we may have injected into these events is again made uncertain, for the end of the day's performance is a dance of men clothed in the skins of leopards and tigers, and having no clear connection with the preceding drama.

The ceremonial of the second day begins with a repetition of the dance of the black-hatted priests with all their daemonical paraphernalia, as on the previous morning. The Skushok enters, preceded by musicians and other attendants. He mounts his throne and is vested, wearing again his rich robes of Chinese silk; but to-day his head is covered by the tall red hat, the red hat of the great Pandits, supposed to have been introduced in the earliest days of lamaism and certainly of a very ancient pattern. The image cut up on the previous afternoon clearly was intended to be wearing a similar hat. The courtyard fills with people standing pressed together, and the ritual of the lamas below the Skushok's throne is obscured by the crowd. The lamas begin to throw consecrated barley over everyone, and anyone who can obtain the grain treasures it, for it carries good fortune to the house into which it is brought. Presently the entire congregation starts to file past the Skushok, to receive the blessing of the gift of life and the life-giving sacramental food [10] which is administered by attendant lamas. The blessing is given by the Skushok himself; he touches the bowed head of each man as he passes with an elaborate vase called Tze-bum, the vase of life. This ritual is sacred to the Celestial Buddha, called in Sanskrit, Amitayus, in Tibetan, Tze-pang-med, or life without end, whose gift of life is supposed to be transferred in this way to the votaries. The numerous women in the crowd are not actually touched by the vase; it is held just above their heads. The people then receive the sacrament from another lama, in the form of balls of flour kneaded with sugar and butter, stained red on the outside. Each devotee pays a small fee to the monastery and is given a piece of silk, worn for days on the shoulder, and so distinguishing the votary from the less fortunate people who have been unable to attend. Later on the second day, much of the performance of the first day is repeated; the sacrificial effigy is not represented as bound, but lies flat on the ground.

The great crowd, fortified by the life-giving sacra/ ment that they have received, devote the day following these ceremonies to feasting, and, after spending another night in tents or under the open sky, in the willow thickets on the bank of the stream below the monastery, they return to their homes. The festival has come at a time when the barley, sown a month or two before, is growing up rapidly, irrigated by the water from the melting of the snow on the mountains. This season of growth, between the time of sowing and the time of reaping, is a brief respite from labour in the fields; no other festivals of any importance are held until the winter, when ice-bound streams and frozen soil decree another holiday. The people return to spinning and weaving, to the herding of goats and dzos, to the driving of yaks into the mountain pastures of the highest valleys. Meanwhile the barley grows higher and the grain sets in the ear.

Some of the lamas are occupied in agricultural pur/ suits, supervising the huge estates of the monastery, for Hemis Gonpa is one of the largest landowners in Indian Tibet. But, although the ritual in the gonpa becomes less onerous after the festival, a continuous cycle of religious observances fills the year. Not only must the daily services in the monastic temples be performed, but lamas must also visit shrines far from the gonpa buildings, by the sides of roads, in isolated valleys. There is such a shrine in the valley that leads to the Digar La, a high and little-frequented pass across the Ladak Mountains, north of the Indus valley, somewhat nearer to Leh than to Hemis. Here, just below the great lateral moraines of a vanished glacier, by the side of a stream that descends the steep valley, there stands a single tree, the last tree that the traveller to the north will see for many days. It stands in the corner of an incomplete enclosure, at one side of which there is a rude stone altar. To this place, a party of eight lamas and four attendants brings drums and shawms, service books and barley flour for offerings. On the altar are set perhaps twenty ceremonial cakes of meal, tall flat triangular pieces of brown paste, each decorated with two disks of white. An amulet case is placed among them and the altar is decorated with green sprays of foliage, but there is no image upon it and there is no painted god or sculptured stone at this shrine. Seated beside the stone table that bears all these little flame-shaped cakes, the lamas read their service, accompanied by pipes and drums, and refreshed from the tea bowls in front of them. Tea, soup and other forms of food are provided at the regular daily ceremonies of the lamas; every meal in the gonpa is a religious gathering, every service a sacred meal, whether it be conducted in a dark and frescoed hall before images of daemonic gods and tranquil saints and Buddhas, or in this remote mountain valley between an isolated tree and a rushing stream.

Just east of Hemis the Indus valley contracts, becoming a narrow gorge, all but impassable when the river is high, as it is in summer. The road from Leh, which the pilgrims going to Hemis followed for twenty miles, now turns to the south into a tributary valley. It is an important route, for many caravans traverse it on their journeys between Leh and Lhasa, and traders from Kulu on the southern slopes of the Himalaya, bring tea into Ladak by this road. The lower part of the valley through which the road runs southward is wide and, in places, fertile; there are many barley fields around its villages, and these fields are for the most part the property of Hemis Gonpa. The two chief settlements are called Miru and Gya. The crags above both villages were fortified in ancient times, and above each village there still stands a small chapel served by a single lama and controlled from Hemis.

At Miru, the Skushok of Hemis has a rest house, for in past times he would have taken the road through these villages on his way to Lhasa. Even to-day, some of his possessions are being packed for transport along this or some parallel road into Tibet, for he is undertaking the journey to the Holy City to perform obsequies for his brother who recently died there. The Skushok is directing the preparations for the journey from a small hermitage high up on the mountain side above Hemis Gonpa. The path up to this retreat leads past a stone marked with a slight depression and anointed with butter, as it is supposed that the stone bears the footprint of the Guru Padma-sambhava, the most magical if not the holiest of lamaistic saints. The hermitage lies several hundred feet above the stream of the Hemis valley; water has to be carried up daily by an old East Tibetan woman, who, clinging tenaciously to the fashion of her country, wears on her head a wooden circle painted red and set with turquoises. In this dry retreat, one of the prin-cesses of the royal house of Ladak, a shy mouse-like child of nine years, is passing part of the summer. She wears a red lama's robe and has her hair cropped short, a mode of dress commonly adopted for small children and believed to ward off evil spirits. Below, in the courtyard, men are preparing pack saddles for the horses carrying the supplies and presents that the Skushok must take to Lhasa, but, when he leaves his rocky retreat, he will travel with a small retinue through India, for he prefers this less arduous route to the more direct but difficult journey across Tibet.

Between Miru and Gya, there is a wayside shrine to some local deity,[11] who is served and propitiated twice a month. The shrine consists of a *lha-tho*, a simple heap of stones built up by travellers who choose a white pebble to place upon it. Behind the *lha-tho* on a boulder a face has been crudely drawn with lamp black. The deity seems to be called Jo-mo-kya-mar; perhaps the name means the goddess of fresh butter. Little lumps of flour paste are offered to her, stuck on to the rock in rows above her black rustic face; at the base of the boulder an offering of butter is placed in a horn supported by two stones.

Beyond this rural shrine, at the village of Gya, there are many water mills, worked by small channels that are led parallel to the stream in the valley, but with a less steep gradient, so that, when the water returns to the stream bed through the mill, it must fall several feet. The machinery of such mills, almost entirely made of wood and stone, is ingenious and can be regulated with some accuracy. Each mill consists of a small circular shed of two storeys. It is built by

the edge of the stream bed, so that the conduit that
supplies its motive power is led into the mill just below
the ceiling of the lower chamber. In this chamber is
set a large vertical beam, its lower end free to rotate
on a pivot, its upper projecting through the ceiling
into the chamber above. The lower end of the beam
is armed with a set of wooden blades pointing out-
ward, like spokes from the axle of a wheel, but also
inclined upward a little. The stream of water, entering
the top of the chamber, is directed by a wooden spout
against one side of this crown of blades, so rotating
the vertical beam. One millstone is fixed firmly on
the floor of the upper chamber. Its centre is pierced
by a hole just large enough for the beam which passes
through it to rotate freely. To the top of the beam,
an upper millstone is securely fastened, but, on either
side of the pin that holds the stone fast to the beam,
there are holes through which grain, falling from
above, can pass between the stones. The grain drops
continually from a large conical hopper of basket
work, open at its lower, smaller end, where a little
wooden spout is attached. This spout is set almost
horizontally, so that the basket must be shaken slightly
to procure a steady fall of grain on to the centre of the
upper millstone. One end of a wooden rod is attached firmly to the hopper; the other end of the rod

Plate XIII. Interior of a water mill at Gya.

lies on the upper surface of the rotating stone. The stone has an irregular surface, and the rod, onomato-poeically called *ba-ra-tak*, is continually jerked by the lumpy millstone, moving beneath its lower end, so shaking grain from the spout of the basket. The flour collects around the edge of the lower millstone.

This contrivance, seemingly crude in execution, if elaborate in design, can be adjusted to give different qualities of meal with considerable nicety. The mill is set going by closing a sluice in the bank of the conduit; this sluice allows the water to flow back into the stream without passing through the mill. If there is too much water in the conduit, so that the millstone starts to turn too quickly, the sluice is partly opened and the speed of the machinery reduced. A rope passing through the floor of the upper chamber enables the rotating beam to be raised or lowered, and the upper and lower millstones separated or brought closer together. Finally, the spout of the hopper can be lowered or raised, made more oblique or more hori-zontal, permitting more or less grain to be shaken from it. When coarse meal is required and the stones are well separated, a more rapid stream of grain can be let out from the spout of the hopper than would be possible when the finest flour is being milled.

At the back of the paved floor, where the flour is heaped up, a slab of stone, engraved with the magical tantra *Om mani padme hum*, is set into the wall of the mill. Seen from the surface of the revolving millstone, the letters of the inscription would appear to rotate. As either the turning of prayers in a copper prayer wheel, or the passage of a traveller past the inscribed stones on a mani wall, is thought to result in the offering of supplication, the placing of the inscription by the millstone suggests that the mill is believed, through such relative motion, to produce a stream of prayer as well as a pile of flour.

Above these mills at Gya, there are several ravines deeply cut in the loose filling that the melting of ancient glaciers has deposited in the valley. In one of these, to the west of the village, is the site of an ancient shrine; a little chapel still stands, white but roofless, on the top of a pinnacle of gravel, at the foot of which a group of very ancient chortens, brown and decayed, are weathering into similar though smaller pinnacles of clay. At the entrance of another ravine there is a number of rock shelters, shallow smoke-stained caves cut into the soft filling of the valley, partly blocked by gravel falling from their roofs. Below them on a little natural platform, there stands an elaborate *lha-tho*, a square structure of sun-dried brick, painted red and capped by a dry bush into which weapons have been stuck. Early each year, a great number of people travels to this place, for at such times a man of Gya, whose office is hereditary, puts on a special robe now sealed up in the gonpa that overlooks the village, and, crowned with the five-pointed diadem of a Boddhisattva, becomes possessed for a few hours and prophesies to the crowd, telling the fortunes that the year has in store. But, at this time when the harvest is beginning, the place is deserted; most of the mills are not working, though soon there will be grain enough to supply them all. The first fruits of the barley fields have already been wreathed around pillars in the chapel of the gonpa that stands on a rock overlooking the stream.

At Miru the reaping has disclosed a pattern of zigzag lines among the stubble, apparently tiny irrigation channels that divide the land into innumerable quincuncial lozenges, an arrangement that would have delighted the author of *The Garden of Cyrus*. New straw from these fields has been fashioned into a kite-shaped charm to catch such devils as may attempt to enter the Skushok's rest house. Throughout the whole country of the Upper Indus the villagers are cutting the crop. As the immense harvest moon, hanging high above the snow-covered mountains, whitens the stubble of the newly cut fields, they carry in the sheaves, working all night, filling the whole moon-drenched country with their shouting and song. The year before the harvest failed and many died of starvation, but this season has been exceedingly fruitful and everyone will have enough.

III

LAKES IN THE DESERT

LAKES IN THE DESERT[1]

WHERE the valley of the Indus narrows, the
dry country is sparsely settled, but north and
south of the gorge, lying in a dusty land like
a few remaining stones on a worn-out headdress,
many lakes are scattered. They vary in colour within
a restricted range of blues and greens, just as the turquoises that they resemble differ one from another.
Each shade of blue or green sums up in itself a structure and a history, for each lake is a small world,
making its nature known to the larger world of the
desert most clearly in its colour. These little worlds
of turquoise, set among red, brown, grey and white
rocks, are not independent of the dry landscape around
them; the meaning of their colours is best seen if they
are compared with lakes in other countries where,
among swamps and fertile fields, turquoises are forgotten and their colours replaced by more earthy
yellows and greens.

In the Kashmir valley there are shallow green lakes
full of weeds, which float in the feeble current and
are curved into long sinuous arabesques. On the
shores of these lakes the Mogul emperors and nobles
built their pleasure gardens. Streams rushing down

the Himalayas were diverted to form cascades, or were led to innumerable fountains which sparkled in the summer sun. Around the fountains at evening flowers hung their heads, miming the curves of the spraying water. Fireworks were set off to contribute showers of golden sparks, so that to the ladies daintily crossing the tiny stepping stones between the fountains, their legs cooled by the spray drenching their silk trousers, the world, hemmed in with immense plane trees, seemed constructed solely of cascades of flowers, water and golden rain.

In the early morning, two embankments cutting off a corner of the lake lift a small undulant bridge out of a sea of mist. Far across the water stands a mosque built to contain one of the long red hairs of the Prophet's beard, and here the decorations of the wall assume the same flowery watery pattern that once filled the garden by night and the weedy reaches of the lakes by day. So much are fire, water and flowers needed to complete the decorative scheme of the architecture of the Moguls, that the palaces at Agra and Delhi seem to be but theatrical backdrops built in marble, erected to stage an unending carnival of water and light. Even the ladies-in-waiting could not cross the chamber of their mistress dry-shod, for a fountain in the centre filled a narrow tank that ran along the entire length of her pavilion. In the smaller chambers, the fountains ran perennially with rosewater. The fashion of these palaces in the dry unbroken plain was transported to the mountains of the north in Kashmir. Behind each waterfall in the gardens are niches, which were filled with lights at night. Each drop of falling water was for a moment a minute lens concentrating the brightness of the light behind it, as if to give it strength to penetrate the heavy perfume of the summer air.

On darker mornings, when the rising sun is hidden by storm clouds, and the sparkle of the sinuous ripples around yellow and white water-lilies for a time is lost, the aspect of the lakes in this fertile valley, though changed, is still in accord with the country's fertility. The green vegetation of the marshes, no longer having to compete with a luminous blue above, now seems the source of light in the landscape. Seen through the rain-bearing air, the bright details of the landscape disappear; only the boundaries between the water and air and earth remain, and they become suddenly sharpened. The fountains and trees of the gardens of the Moslem emperors cease to be distinguishable from all the other water and vegetation of the earth. Man is now represented, in this sharp and simplified land-scape, only by great patches of vermilion paint which

glow on a distant hillside, floating between the green
of the swamp and the black of the rain clouds, painted
to honour the stones of the hill, for every one is the
image of a god. But, whether the garden civilisation
of the Mohammedan emperors be temporarily ascen-
dant in the sunlight, or the older colours of the Hindus
be triumphant beneath the rain-pregnant clouds, the
lakes of the Kashmir valley are the lakes of a fertile
country and partake of its fertility. They bear innumerable boats, from which fish are caught in skil-
fully manipulated throw-nets. Weeds are dredged up
to provide fodder for the cattle, and water chestnuts
and lotus roots for human food. And, as if such
fertility were inadequate, sods of marshy earth are
bound together into rafts heavy with manure, and
these are moored in rows across the swamp to form
floating gardens, so that the boundary between earth,
air and water is made fruitful and bears the fiery
red fruits of tomato plants.

South and west, farther into India, there is another
group of lakes, on the Son plateau of the Salt Range
in the Punjab. The country here is dry, but can be
cultivated in terraces; small villages are built on low
hills among the terraced fields. The largest of the
lakes here, Son Sakesar Kahar, the "ocean lake of the
Son plateau", lies below such a village, called Chitta,

perched on a little cliff. This site is extremely ancient. Half a mile from the cluster of white houses, the rudest sort of stone tools made from flakes of cherty limestone have been discovered in a layer of ancient soil. To those who know this, the place is invested with a haunted feeling, that could never be felt by the peasants who work in the fields around the village, however superstitious they may be. The lake at first must have had an outflow, but since the early men made their tools near its shore, it has successively swollen and fallen, and now lies shrunken below the cliff on which the modern village stands. From a little distance, on a clear still day, the water seems like a dull mirror set in a white expanse of salty mud, its surface reflecting the pale sky, the terraced hills and the little white houses of Chitta on its north shore and of Uchhali to the south. But, when the white-crusted mud is crossed, and, at the edge of the lake its own colour is revealed, Son Sakesar Kahar appears as the centre from which the dead, haunted feeling of the whole country is diffused. The water is of a dull opaque pink colour; along the edge, separating this pink from the white of the salt flat, is a narrow band of intensely green scum, where a small flock of flamingos feeds. They seem to unite in their plumage the white of the shore and the pink of the water, that the green scum of algae strives to keep apart. The full power of this extraordinary arrangement of colours is not felt until, in the centre of the lake, the sanguineous waves grow, beating against the prow of a boat, and the rush of not yet visible hailstones is heard as they fly through the air from a darkened sky. Then, though the shore is but a mile or two distant, the world is transformed into a dead and empty plane, its waters turned to blood; all familiar things seem to have become irrelevant objects thrown together in a meaningless assortment, while one black insignificant air-filled boat, with its cargo of bottles, thermometers and pieces of wire, struggles blindly against the wind.

In the quality of this scene, accentuated by the foetid sulphurous water that lies at the bottom of the lake, may be traced the whole life of the surrounding country, as surely as in the lakes of the fruitful valley of Kashmir. As vegetation and the refuse of human occupation decay in a basin around a lake, some of the products of the decomposition are carried into the lake by rain and water seeping through the soil. These materials, compounds of nitrogen and phosphorus, become incorporated into the substance of the minute plants that grow and multiply in the sunlight and give their green colour to the lakes of damp and fertile lands. As the Son plateau became dryer and the lake below Chitta receded from its ancient shore, such materials must have been continually added to its water. When the water finally ceased to flow from the old outlets, the nutrient materials that reached the lake must have accumulated; the lake then doubtless became opaque and green with microscopic life. Khabakki Kahar, a smaller, shallower, less salt lake eight miles to the east, is in such a condition to-day, its waters heavy with minute greenish plants. But, with the fertilising products of decay, salt and soda also entered the lake and likewise could not be washed from it; so that, as the water became more fruitful, the variety of species that could utilise its abundance became restricted, and to-day it seems that only a minute powdery plant, whose name, *Lamprocystis roseo-persicina*, inappropriately recalls the Mogul emperors, can survive in the salt and alkaline water, which it clouds with aggregates of pink cells. If the lake escapes the remote vicissitudes that threaten it, earth movements and futile attempts to employ its saline waters for irrigation, it will grow in bitterness, each year collecting more salt and soda, so that finally, though more loaded with fertilising material than even to-day, it will become sterile on account of its saltness, the pink colour will depart, and no living thing, save a few bacteria, remain.

Forces similar to those acting in these low-lying lakes, but acting with different intensities, also control the colours of the turquoise lakes of the Tibetan Plateau. But here, in a cold and barren country, less of the nutritive substances are brought into the lake basins. In some of the deeper lakes the crop of micro-scopic vegetation is not large enough to modify greatly the blue colour of pure water. In other smaller lakes, the water is coloured a clear luminous green by the clouds of tiny plants inhabiting it. But in the waters filling the mountain basins, scooped out of rock or glacial gravel, yellowish and earthy shades are never found, for these colours are produced by matter leached out of swampy ground; nor do such lakes ever exhibit the fantastic and abnormal hue of the over-nourished and over-salted Son Sakesar Kahar.

Above Leh several roads diverge, leaving the Indus valley, to rejoin as they approach the turquoise lakes of the desert. The roads cross the Ladak mountains by different snow-covered passes, and the two chief descending tracks unite at a small village called Tangtse, a few miles west of the great blue lake Pang-gong Tso. Tangtse is approached through a wide barren valley; the few houses that constitute the village seem to hide behind a little grove of willow trees planted on one side of a stream, as if these trees were

the greatest treasure of a place that wished to put up
a brave front, a green and damp façade, to the hostile
dry world before it. Beyond the willow grove a small
monastery, surrounded by ruined walls of mud, stands
at the foot of a rocky slope. On the other side of the
stream there is no irrigation, and the wide plain of the
valley is littered with granite boulders. The freshly
broken surfaces of this granite are white, but the whiteness is for the most part hidden by the rich brown
patina with which the boulders are covered. Unshaded by willow trees, they have surrendered to the
desert. But it seems that the place is not now dry
enough to allow the formation of this bronzed and
polished crust, for, where the patina has flaked away,
it is not replaced; here and there patches of the solid
naked whiteness of the granite are revealed by the
breaking of the brown skin. The period of extreme
aridity that has caused the formation of the patina has
left its traces elsewhere, as is shown by a stone flake
picked up at Kargil[2] on the western borders of Indian
Tibet, where the same climatic changes must have
occurred. This flake of greenish trap was first worked
by palaeolithic man; at a later time, lying on the surface
of a terrace above the Wakka river, it acquired a rich
reddish ochraceous crust. Then the flake was refashioned as a scraper and left on the terrace where it

was found. But, since the time of the reworking of the tool, no patina has formed; the new chipped surfaces still have the greenish black colour of the trap rock of which the flake is made. The patina of the boulders at Tangtse was doubtless formed at the same time as that of the stones on the terraces at Kargil. Perhaps this single implement shows that this time was before the men of the country had given up the use of stone tools. But the history of Tangtse has not been recorded only by changes in the weather; men have written and drawn on the boulders, cutting through their brown crust, and have in this manner engraved the history of events, which, if less monumental than the great secular changes of climate, might seem more poignant if we fully understood them. Among all the rocks lying beyond the stream, one great square block stands out, even at a great distance. It is to this block that the willows must give way, as representing the true genius and treasure of the place. On the north face of the rock, looking toward the village across the stream, nothing has been drawn or written. The other faces tell fragments of unsuspected stories. Cut into the patina of the south face is a large cross rising from a very simplified flower; above the cross a word is engraved, to its left, vertical columns of a long inscription.[3] The language is Sogdhian, an

Iranian tongue spoken in the middle ages in Christian and Buddhistic cities of Central Asia; it is not other-wise known as far south as this. The long inscription records the journey of a man from Samarkand, his name unfortunately illegible, who reached Tangtse in two hundred and fifteen stages on his way to Tibet. The short word above the cross appears to be the name Jesus. The letters are very white and quite unpatinated, though they cannot have been cut later than the four-teenth century. On the west side of the rock is another cross and another short inscription. This inscription, written in the Tokharian language and script, is of two words only, *tane wewimarusisi*. The word *tane* means "here"; *wewimarusisi* is known nowhere else and no meaning for it can be conjectured. That the writers of these inscriptions were Christians, pre-sumably Nestorians, is certain; one of them at least came from Samarkand and was travelling to Tibet; more than this cannot be surmised. Perhaps the writers were fleeing from Moslem persecution; perhaps somewhere in Tibet there are other crosses and other inscriptions recording that journey.

On the eastern face of the rock, these Christian travellers have again engraved the name of Jesus, but here no longer among crosses. It is surrounded by Buddhistic symbols, chortens, swastikas and

geometrical designs, and by scenes of huntsmen enjoy-
ing the chase. The only other writing on this rock is
a Tibetan date, "the year of the earth-tiger". The
writing seems to be not later than the thirteenth century; the mode of recording the date is based on the
sixty-year cycle, apparently not otherwise employed in
Indian Tibet until the sixteenth century, though of
ancient use in China. Between this unfixed record
of a year and the name of the Son of God, obscurely
cut in the warm patina of the forgotten desert, ibex,
yak and two fine stags are pursued by hunters armed
with bows and slings. These men appear to be ob-
taining food and clothing, oblivious of the symbols
and letters scattered around them, where the name of
Christ lies among the cenotaphs of Gautama. No
crucifix sprouts from between the horns of these stags,
nor do the crowns of their antlers bear the crescent
of Artemis, whose own herb *Artemisia* grows between
the snow and the desert. Though the hunter slings his
stone at the stag merely to bring home meat and a skin
for a new pair of shoes, yet in this country of the ibex,
wild sheep and yak, the very presence of stags drawn
on the rock raises a question. Around Tangtse the
valleys are too dry for deer to inhabit them, and no
deer are found until the forests of Kashmir are reached
a hundred miles to the west. It seems unlikely that

the hunt took place so far away; possibly after the desert conditions created the patina, there was a time wetter than the present, and then a few deer may have ventured into the country and established themselves here and there in these valleys. There is no other record of this, and the great rock at Tangtse, like a shapeless Sphinx, guards the treasure of its knowledge jealously, asking more questions than curiosity and patience can answer.

Beyond the rock the road to the east follows the stream, which rushes between narrow strips of pasture, where a fine incrustation of soda effloresces between the scanty blades of grass. Snow trout breed in this stream, and numberless fish lurk in the deep holes in the angle of every bend.

Where the pasture is widest, there is a small village called Mugleb, and beyond this the stream narrows, rising as an indefinite trickle in the flat head of the valley. The watershed so formed is hardly noticed as it is crossed, and above the source of the stream, flat pan-like basins fill the valley, so uncertain is the direction of the drainage. One of these, called Tsar Tso, seems now to contain water permanently. It is a tiny grey weedy lake, but on this road it is the first of the many hundred that stud the Tibetan plateau, collecting and evaporating its scant supply of brackish water; the other hollows beyond Tsar Tso are usually only filled with dry silt. Poor turquoises, for the most part lost and their places marked with a little dust, yet, for the traveller from the west, they are the first set out on the dusty background of the desert. Beyond the pans of silt the valley narrows and then, suddenly turning a corner, bends a little to the north, to open into a great rift. Its walls are brown, white, purple, dull red, sage green, burnt colours, as if the earth has been a furnace for the firing of the band of blue enamel, Panggong Tso, a lake forty miles long, which drains the waters of more inaccessible lakes to the east.

As the summer comes slowly and the last snow of June falls so stilly, the sky becomes filled with a grey down that fades, breaking into separate powdery flakes. From the centre of the lake, the dry burnt colours of the shore are lost completely; the snow falls on the enamelled surface, silently strikes it and rests for a moment, then disappears. In the blue water small black spots move leisurely here and there, and still tinier bright red points can be seen skipping among them, as if the turquoise had suddenly lique-fied like the miraculous blood of a saint, while into the liquid blue, tiny pieces of its black matrix and minute particles of red ironstone had floated. In the deeper water and along the shore, small pale shrimps skurry about. These three crustacea, black, red and pale grey, are the only animals that normally live in the lake. Fish occasionally may enter its saline waters, but they do not establish themselves. Their proper homes are the small lagoons that fringe the lake, and the stream that enters its western end, and the pools in the swampy estuary of that stream.

The fish of the stream are snow trout of two kinds, both found throughout the country and distributed far to the east into Nepal and to the north-west in the Pamir mountains. In the lagoons and pools two peculiar species of loaches are found, restricted to this district and known only from the immediate vicinity of the lake and the valley toward Tangtse, by which the lake is approached. The ancestors of these fish must have had a strange history, dependent on the changes that the lake itself has suffered.

As the snow clears and the surface of the lake is blown up into white-capped waves by a strong after-noon wind, the shore can be seen extending for miles below the walls of the narrow depression, brown and white and purple, dull red and sage green. Barren stony fans spread out from the subsidiary valleys; along the south shore the mountains bear a row of small glaciers like tongues stuck out in the manner of the customary Tibetan salutation. But for ice so

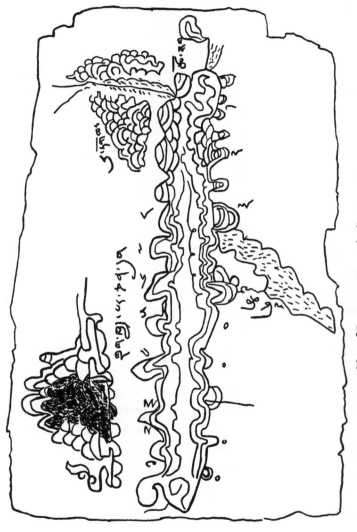

Map of Panggong Tso and adjacent country.

to offer its soul to a thirsty traveller across the blue salt water of the lake seems an act of mockery.

Below the level of the glacier snouts, where a rocky spur projects toward the lake between two valleys, wave-cut terraces can be seen here and there. Some lie just above the present level of the water, others several hundred feet above the turquoise lake. If the basin were filled to these higher levels, several lakes, including Tso Nyak to the east and Pangur Tso to the south, would be joined to form one. The saline waters of Panggong Tso would be freshened, for an outlet would flow toward the west. Such a condition was established late during the Ice Age, when the glaciers that filled the Panggong valley had retreated, though the smaller glaciers on the mountains were

---

The map opposite was made by two Ladakis, bSod-nams-dar-rgyas and Thse-dban-bkra-shis, who were sent to make zoological collections in Tso Nyak. The original, drawn in pencil on corrugated wrapping cardboard, is unsuited to photographic reproduction, but the ink-tracing here used is reasonably accurate. It is of great interest as it indicates how deeply the scroll-work and linear rhythms of modern Tibetan painting have impressed themselves on the minds of the villagers. The name Thso-nyag is entered on the extreme right of the map, but as the two Ladakis only saw its western end, they have represented the lake itself as being far too small. The broad valley running south from the shore of Panggong Tso presumably connected that lake with Pangur Tso during interglacial times. Pangur Tso is not shown on the map, but lies immediately east of this valley, south of the eastern end of Panggong Tso.

again to advance a little. The great lake so formed stretched from the hidden eastern basins Tso Nyak and Tso Rum in Tibet, westward over Tsar Tso and its empty neighbours, filling the Tangtse valley with water, and to the south over another large and now closed lake, Pangur Tso. This huge interglacial lake was fresh and far richer in animal life than is the present Panggong Tso. Countless water snails have left their shells in deposits laid down on its bottom. These shells, now dead and white, washed from the lacustrine clay in which they were embedded, are cast up on the shore of the present lake, where handfuls may be picked up from the strand of a quiet bay. The first travellers to study the region, misled by this jetsam, believed these white shells to belong to snails living in the modern lake. The shallower marginal water of the ancient lake must have been full of water weeds, though none lives in Panggong to-day, for, with the shells, beds of ribbon-like leaves are found, and these, cast on the beach, also give a misleading impression of living abundance below the turquoise surface. Among these weeds, shoals of fish must have swum; one species is now found in both Tso Nyak and Pangur Tso, where the weed still survives, a relic of their previous continuity. This lake-loving fish, however, seems unable to survive in the lagoons and pools that fringe Panggong Tso itself. But the loaches found in these pools and lagoons, and even in the little pools in the valley near Tangtse, carry in their bodies evidence that they too are descended from the fish of the ancient lake. Unlike the loaches of flowing water, so common in the streams of Central Asia, they have large air-filled swim bladders, enabling them to adjust their position in deep still water. Such structures have been lost in the species living in streams and in the shallow lakes of Kashmir; that they are found in the loaches of the pools around Panggong Tso shows that these fishes developed in the large deep lake that covered their present habitats. Through-out its entire basin, wherever fresh and quiet waters still exist, the ancient lake has left not only dead shells and dry wave-cut cliffs, but this living testimony of its former vast extent. Long before the rock at Tangtse received the dark brown polish in which the crosses were cut, these little fish must have swum over its site.

This large lake receded; glaciers advanced toward the present water-level, formed moraines and receded again. The melting back of these glaciers may have filled the lakes a little, forming some of the lower beaches. The very dry period probably occurred subsequent to this. Since then the water-level has

oscillated up and down; in the middle of the nine-
teenth century the lake fell so low that a rocky islet
stuck out five feet above the water, only to be submerged again when the lake rose after the rainy years
at the end of the century. At the time of the very
dry period, Tsar Tso could hardly have escaped complete desiccation. This period must have been a difficult one for the fish, unable to live in the salt and
barren water of Panggong Tso and ill-suited to life
in the rapid streams which, though reduced in volume,
no doubt still ran in the upper parts of the valley.
The fish must have survived here and there in pools,
probably in the estuary at the north-west end of the
lake. Perhaps the stags engraved on the granite
boulder indicate a succeeding damper time, a happier
age for these fish which were again able to spread
into their old haunts and recolonise the pools of the
valleys that had once been lakes and then had become
deserts. The rock continues to ask questions which as
yet cannot be answered; the crosses here converse of
fishes as surely as a fish engraved on a rock has elsewhere been used to epitomise the history of the Cross.

North of Panggong Tso, twenty miles from its
extreme western end, and perched over half a mile
higher in the rarefied air, is a group of small lakes,
filling basins cut in the rocks by glaciers, or lying

behind the moraines from which these glaciers have retreated. The largest of these lakes is called Ororotse Tso. Even in summer it is ice-bound, so that from the pass by which it is approached from the south the whole surface of the water seems covered with a tightly drawn milky sheet. In July the ice melts a little at the edge of the lake. The marginal and exposed water, warmed slightly, becomes denser than the ice and flows beneath it, melting the white sheet from below, so that, while its upper surface is so smooth, underneath it is sculptured into thousands of spikes and icicles, hanging into the green water of the lake like stalactites, to be perceived only by touch when an arm is thrust through a hole made in the ice in the middle of the lake. Below lies the greenish water, in which tiny red crustacea swim, more numerous than in the turquoise Panggong Tso, for here, in this shallow lake, the greenness of the water indicates that there is an abundant supply of food. Even on the bottom, forty feet below the ice, there is a carpet of simple greenish plants, among which bloodworms, thousands in a square yard, browse on the bacteria and decaying vegetable matter of the mud. This ice-covered lake, so high in the mountains, surrounded by snow-covered rock below which sparse tufts of grass grow in the damper places, seems to provide a

richer and more pullulant habitat for such animals as
can live in its icy waters, than any of the other lakes
of the country. In other regions, such as the Alps,
where lakes may be almost perpetually ice-bound,
such numbers of animals do not manage to exist.
Perhaps the way in which the Tibetan mountains
have been eroded to form fans of rock detritus, now
only washed by small streams that percolate through
much finely broken gravel, gives to this inflowing
water the greatest possible opportunity of dissolving
materials needed by the microscopic plants of the lake.
In this way, the desert surrenders its fertility to what
little water may flow through it.

Each summer day, as the sun at noon rises higher
into the pale sky, and a little more of the ice at the
edge of Ororotse Tso is melted, more and more heat
is also supplied to the surfaces of the other lakes,
Panggong Tso and Pangur, Mitpal Tso, Yaye Tso
and Khyagar Tso, and Tso Moriri, the deepest of
them all, each one lying south of its predecessor. These
lakes have lost their sheets of ice early in the summer,
probably at the beginning of June. Since then, save
when snowstorms have obscured the sun, their upper
waters have been warmed a little each day.

In the early morning as the sun rises, a light breeze
may blow over Panggong Tso, raising the surface into

little waves of lapis lazuli, whose crests are gilded by
the almost horizontal sunbeams; or blowing less
strongly, the breeze may merely make large ripples
that draw out the reflections of the mountains into
long pseudopodia of snow and granite. As the
morning becomes hotter, the breeze dies away, leaving
the surface of the lake quite undisturbed. The shore-
line, seen across the water, is lifted up by a mirage,
until, reaching the level of some dry and ancient
beach, it seems that the ghost of one of the past lakes
has appeared above the flat blue surface. In the afternoon a stiffer wind blows; the waves break into crests
in the evening light, as the long mountain shadows
grow across the wide mouths of the valleys on the
distant shore, beyond the white-spotted water. During
the first days of summer these winds have mixed the
newly warmed water with the cooler water below it,
carrying some of its heat into regions where it cannot
radiate away by night. The currents set up by the
wind may at first perhaps reach to the deepest parts of
the basins, and in the shallower lakes they warm the
water even at the bottom. As summer advances the
sun daily rises higher into the sky and snowstorms
become less frequent. The surface water now behaves
as a cork floating in a bowl, which can only be submerged when a definite amount of work is done upon

it. A time soon comes when the water, expanding as it is warmed, becomes so light that the force of the wind can no longer drive it to the bottom.

Throughout the greater part of the summer, only the upper layers of water, perhaps twenty or thirty feet, are mixed by the wind, and the lower regions are isolated from the upper by a layer in which the temperature is found to change very rapidly when a thermometer is dropped to increasingly greater depths. Above, the warmer well-mixed water is continually brought in contact with the air; below, there is a cold region of decay, cut off from the outer world, and not restored to it until the autumn, when the cold nights chill the surface waters more than the enfeebled sun can warm them by day. Then the whole structure, slowly elaborated by the wind several months before, is toppled over before the lake begins to freeze.

On this seasonal cycle of stratification and overturn, much of the character of a lake depends. In the deep blue lakes, such as Panggong Tso and Tso Moriri, where the amount of microscopic vegetation is not great enough to colour the water, the cold layers at the bottom of the lake remain relatively unchanged throughout the summer months. Few dead organisms fall to the bottom and little material is added to the mud by the decay of beings that have lived in the

water above. In such lakes there is always an abundant supply of oxygen, even in the greatest depths;
animals can breathe in such a habitat, and if they do
not colonise it in numbers, it is because there is so
little to eat. In the shallower greener lakes, where the
warmer surface layers are filled with the powdery cells
of microscopic plants, so much decaying matter falls
to the bottom that the deepest water, in contact with a
richly nutritive mud, is quickly robbed of its oxygen.
In the summer the lower half of such a lake becomes
an anaerobic microcosm shut off from the world of
air above; no animals can survive in its dark and
sulphurous water. In few of the lakes of these high
regions do enough of the dead bodies of microscopic
plants fall to the bottom to deplete the cold deep water
entirely of its oxygen. In the deepest part of Khyagar
Tso there is no oxygen, and the mud almost seventy
feet below the surface is made up of the flocculent
masses of dying plants and the cast skins of crustacea,
a nutrient mass that must be left untasted throughout
the summer months. At the bottom of Mitpal Tso
and Yaye Tso, the balance between breathing and
feeding is more nicely adjusted, so that here worms,
the red larvae of gnats and small bivalves can live in
the deepest water which never becomes completely
devoid of oxygen, while the more fertile green layers

of the surface continually drop food from above into these dark, cold and plantless waters.

The green plant cells in the surface waters, building up their bodies in the sunlight from simple inanimate materials, are eaten by the red copepods and the larger blackish waterfleas. In some of the lakes, small shrimps, called scientifically *Gammarus*, swim in the open water and in turn capture the dark lumbering *Daphnia*. But here the cycle ends; when the *Gammarus* die they fall to the bottom of the lake and their bodies decay, so returning to the water the matter of which they are made. In this, the largest predatory animals in the water are like "the Ichthyophagi or fish-eating nations about Ægypt" who "affected the Sea for their grave: thereby declining visible corruption, and restoring the debt of their bodies".[4] Where fish have managed to invade a lake in Indian Tibet, the clumsy black *Daphnia* is never found; it would be too easy a prey, and was doubtless eaten up long ago. The *Gammarus* too are more wary, keeping to the margins where there is plenty of cover. The fish themselves feed chiefly on grubs in the shallow littoral water, and die where they have lived; the debt of bodies is restored, for few are ever removed from the lake. One or two may be captured by the Tibetan tern, whose lovely form, so perfectly made for life over the ocean, seems curiously misplaced among the dry mountains.

To the Kashmiris, the lakes of their valleys are a rich storehouse from which they can supply their daily needs; perhaps the pink and dying Son Sakesar Kahar was of equal importance to the prehistoric people of the Salt Range Plateau. But the high Central Asiatic lakes remain for the most part outside the lives of the few people who inhabit the country around them. Though they are less sterile than the lakes of the highest parts of the Alps and of other high and wet mountains, they never produce such aquatic harvests as are gathered in from the valley lakes of Kashmir. The lake fishes are never caught for food by man. They are too small, too scarce, perhaps too sacred. They are only common in Pangur Tso; in Yaye Tso a few young loaches may be found. The vicissitudes of the fishes in the lagoons around Panggong Tso have already been described. In other lakes they were probably unable to survive great climatic changes, so that they may have disappeared from waters in which once they were able to exist.

At the end of winter the people of Man, on the southern shore of Panggong Tso, use its frozen surface as an easy highway by which they can cross the lake; at that time only can they fetch the stumps of willow

trees from the sheltered Nyagtzu valley on the northern
shore, to replenish their scanty supply of fuel. But
the Tibetans have not been blind to the beauty of the
turquoise waters. Perhaps following some Indian pre-
cedent, lamaistic tradition regards the shore of a lake
as the most propitious place for the building of a
gonpa. In the arid mountains, the lake basins are in
general so devoid of the necessities of life that the
injunction is seldom carried out in these regions. There
is a small monastery at Korzok, above the blue snow-
reflecting water of Tso Moriri, in a village made up
of a few houses and tents on a small fan, and reputed
to be the most elevated agricultural settlement in the
world. There is another monastery, even less important, at Merak on the shores of Panggong Tso. These
seem to have been built chiefly to minister to the
spiritual needs of the remote communities grouped
around them. Only in the Tso Kar basin, west of
Tso Moriri, is a tiny gonpa found, seemingly remote
from secular traffic, whose site may have been determined by the traditional appropriateness of the place.
The Tso Kar depression contains two lakes, one fresh
water, the other very salt. A few Chang-pa, or
nomads, have their tents on the rich pasture at the
edge of the fresh-water lake. Yellowish brown and
dark grey snow-capped mountains form a ring around

the basin, broken only in the south by a dull crimson hill. Cut into their bases lie row upon row of ancient beaches, encircling the entire depression and set one on the other like a flight of steps. From high up on the side of the basin, the lakes, reflecting the sky, seem blue, though when more closely examined their water is green. Within the ancient shore lines a girdle of pasture surrounds the fresh-water lake Sta-tsa-puk Tso, the lake of horse-grazing, while a girdle of salt sur-rounds Tso Kar, the white lake. The highest of the ancient beaches has cut into the rock on the eastern side of the basin, forming a broad shelf, on which stands a tiny white gonpa or a chapel, below which both the green-encircled and the white-encircled lakes can be seen. There is no permanent settlement for miles, though the track that skirts the lakes is one of the routes between Leh and Lhasa. Beyond Tso Kar a large white chorten stands by the road; at its side a rough throne has been built, so that a travelling Skushok or other dignitary can rest here for an hour or two.

As the sun sets, the yellowish brown and dark grey mountains, the blue-green lake in the distance, the dull crimson hill, even the young crescent moon, each takes on its peculiar shade of pearly twilight grey; only the chorten remains white and solid as night spreads into the valley.

Mountain chains and desert valleys lie between the lakes. So little rain falls in these valleys that, without the mountains, the whole country would be a desolate waste. But the cold peaks condense from the air such moisture as it possesses, adding continually to their glaciers and fields of snow. The snouts of the glaciers slowly descend under their ever-increasing load, or melt back in times of exceptional sunshine. From the snow and ice on the mountains, small streams flow into the lakes or coalesce to form larger rivers which carry the once-frozen waters down to the Indus. Some of these glacier streams, running only after the hot afternoons of summer, die in a bed of gravel and stones. The vertical diversity of the climate makes human life possible in Indian Tibet. To the east, where the mountain ranges die out and are replaced by the high Tibetan plateau, the country is too dry for any sort of permanent settlement. Over large tracts of country water can only be obtained in winter, by the melting of snow. In a few favoured places there may be a little pasture, which the Chang-pa nomads share with the Tibetan antelope and the wild ass.

The wide valley of the Chang-chenmo river, lying north of the lakes that have been described, runs from the edge of the Tibetan plateau, collecting water from side streams supplied by the mountains that rise higher

and higher on either side of the river as it descends
to the west. The hills that flank the Chang-chenmo
are yellowish grey, with great patches of crimson and
blue-grey rock. Though the colours seem more fiery
than those of the Panggong depression to the south,
this is a deceptive appearance. The rocks here have
suffered less during the violent upheavals which built
the mountain ranges. Many still contain recognisable
fossils, the remains of animals that lived on the coral
reefs flourishing in the warm waters of the ancient
sea, an eastern extension of the Mediterranean, to
which the name Tethys is given. The side valleys that
run into the western part of the Chang-chenmo are
very deep; that by which the icy waters of Ororotse
Tso drain, is blocked by steep moraines and is almost
impassable. Somewhat further to the east there is a
path which runs through the sheltered and more accessible valley of a tributary stream towards a patch
of grass called Pamzal. Grass is so precious that each
piece of pasture has a name. This tributary stream
swells each summer afternoon, as the day's load of
melted ice is delivered into it. Its valley is dry, but
is perhaps better watered by the periodic rise and fall
of the stream than is the more open Chang-chenmo
valley. It is warm and well protected from the wind,
so that it seems more like a sandy garden than a desert.

The vegetation is not continuous, but the sheltered spots are gay with flowers. The yellow spikes of *Corydalis moorcroftiana* seem like golden showers that spring from green and leafy fountains. In the hot air of midday, lacy winged insects like ant lions are found flying over the sandy soil, creatures that to the naturalist from the north give to the place a sub-tropical appearance. A few miles further on, where the valley spreads out to join the Chang-chenmo at Pamzal, the colours of the landscape are still bright but are inanimate, the red and dull blue of the rock, the white of the snow peaks to the north.

The Chang-chenmo river is shallow, and flows in a wide valley that provides little protection from the violent winds sweeping through it. The flood plain is for the most part stony, but is here and there covered with bushes of *Myricaria elegans*, a dry shrub allied to the tamarisk. More rarely there are small areas of pasture. A few men drive their yaks up to these patches of grass in the summer; some of the herdsmen are said to come from Khalatse beyond Leh, a journey of more than a hundred miles. The valley, however, is generally deserted; a cold hearth, or a *lha-tho* on a rock above the river, alone indicates that men have lived here for a time.

Above the flood plain the sides of the valley are

barren; in the driest parts there are long stretches of gravel on which single *Christolea* plants, spaced per- haps a hundred feet apart, may be found growing. Where a gully descends, cutting across the gravel, isolated plants of wild but quite edible rhubarb, can be found in its stony bottom. Above the gravel, on the lower slopes of the hills, the vegetation, though still sparse, is a little more abundant; the cruciferous *Christolea*, bearing heads of white four-petalled flowers on lanky stems, is replaced by a more important plant, *Eurotia ceratoides*, here called bur-tse, a dry shrubby herb whose woody roots, stretching desperately into the arid hillside and dug out only with much effort, are extensively used for fuel. The wild asses canter un- disturbed on these slopes. Immune by law and cus- tom, they are regarded as unclean by the Tibetans, who never taste their excellent meat. The skins are sometimes used for making shoes, but any shoes made of the hide of an ass or a horse must be removed on entering a gonpa. Shoes of other material need not be taken off, for the Tibetan Buddhists, unlike the Indians, bare their heads and not their feet when entering a sacred place.

Higher up the mountain slope, at a level to which the snouts of small glaciers descend, and where the snow must lie far into the summer, the vegetation changes for a second time, the bur∕tse giving place to a grey aromatic plant, a small species of wormwood called *Artemisia minor*, which here covers the hillside. Between its tufts a leguminous plant called *Oxytropis* is found growing, bearing occasional purple flowers. The *Artemisia* runs up the mountain side towards the patches of permanent snow, gradually becoming stunted and sparse until it disappears. A little higher up only a few straggling plants of any sort can exist.

This definite pattern, in which the abundant vegeta∕ tion is confined to a single restricted zone on the hill∕ side, is doubtless the expression of a balance between the warmer drier conditions in the valley and the cold but damper conditions of the mountain peaks. On this balance many of the other living beings of the Chang∕chenmo valley depend. On the stony desert stretches and on the lower sparsely covered slopes where the bur∕tse grows, a few flies and bees can be seen, but no insects seem attached to the few plants that live in such places, or are found running on the gravelly wastes between the plants. In the high belt a pale green plant bug is found feeding on the *Artemisia*, and several species of beetles are associated with the purple∕flowered *Oxytropis*. Higher up the mountain, food for these insects disappears.

At about the level of the thickest vegetation the

mountains tend to project between the valleys as shoulders, which culminate in long level ridges. These ridges are the remains of an ancient valley floor carved by a river before the last upheaval of the country. Around a projecting pinnacle, set precariously on the sharp edge of such a ridge, like a castellated tower, butterflies may be seen flying in circles, as if they had tried to fly continually upward and yet keep always near the ground, until, following the slope to this pinnacle, they were trapped by their behaviour into flitting around it. Unable to break with the ground, they seem prevented from following the main slope to the mountain top, two thousand feet above them. Here may be found a small white butterfly confined to the Karakorum and called *Baltia*, a name derived from the country of the Baltis to the west of Indian Tibet. And with this endemic but undistinguished-looking form, flies the lordly *Kailasius charltonius*, a magnificent creature, white and black with the edges of the red eyespots on its wings delicately shadowed with blue. The curious habit of flying upward on a slope, never far from the ground, seems the possession of a number of kinds of insects. Many individuals may thus be led far above the limits of vegetation; some no doubt ultimately fall prey to spiders[5] lurking in crevices or under fragments of talus among the snow. These spiders probably feed more frequently on springtails and mites, themselves subsisting on minute fragments of dead vegetation carried up by the wind. In these ways, the domain of animal life extends up the mountains somewhat above that of the plant world on which it ultimately depends.

Further to the east, higher up the Chang-chenmo river, the mountains rise less steeply. The sides of the valley are formed by long stretches of more gently undulating hills. The lower slopes are covered with bur-tse; higher up, at about seventeen thousand feet, the grey aromatic *Artemisia* again appears. In damper or more sheltered corners, other gayer plants are found; dandelions grow on a stream bank; a stony slope may be covered with *Delphinium*, bearing the largest flowers that any kind of plant manages to produce in this region.

The best grazing in the upper Chang-chenmo is at a place called Kyam, where there is a wide and swampy pasture. Just outside the limits of this upland meadow, separated from it by a few hundred feet of gravel, there lies a group of hot springs. The calcareous waters of these springs have built up cup-like basins raised above the surrounding plain, and, overflowing these, have watered the gravelly plain into producing a little green grass. Seen through the flickering air over the gravel, green and white flames seem to rise from the earth. Up the valley, behind yellow hills and the dull crimson rock beyond them, a curious mountain stands, cut by three ridges into deep valleys, each ridge yellow and grey in arching horizontal bands. Still further away, fringed by blackish mountains, the Tibetan plateau recedes to the east for a thousand miles.

The pastures of Kyam are the beginning of the home of the Tibetan antelope or *Pantholops*, a peculiar beast, not closely related to any other animal. It is an old inhabitant of the plateau; fossils of a hardly dissimilar form have been found at Hundes to the east. In parts of Tibet, where the antelope is rare or absent and known chiefly from hearsay, it has been confused with the unicorn of tradition and depicted in drawings, as it may be seen appearing in profile, with a single horn. Even in these western parts, where the beast is well known and where no doubt can be entertained about its structure, it seems to have acquired some of the mythology of the fabulous unicorn. It is said that in the old days the antelope was so delighted at the sight of a virgin that it would come and put its nose in her lap.[6] In this way the animal could be easily caught. The story brings back memories of the tapestries in the Cluny and reconstructs itself in the mind as a series of scenes.

Very early in the morning a man in an old robe, and a girl at his side, make their way from a camp they have established by the green grass below the hot spring. They cross the stream just as the day begins and make their way up the valley to the grass where the *Pantholops* are feeding. The beasts are a long way off when the man leaves the child seated and retires into a gully. For an hour the antelopes continue eating the sweet grass at the edge of the river, and the sun slowly rises. The grass perhaps tastes less sweet, for they begin to get restive, moving a little up the valley flank toward the mountain. Hitherto they have looked at the girl only to keep at a safe distance while feeding; now a magnificent buck, well fed and having satisfied the delight of his palate, lets his eyes turn to the girl and take pleasure in her. He wanders from the rest of the beasts, hesitantly moving toward the girl. The other antelopes get panic-stricken and bolt into the hills. The sun is mounting in the sky and in the upper air there are innumerable ice crystals, so that the sun has a halo like the moon on a warm damp night. The buck looks back, realising that all the other beasts have fled, but he cannot take his eyes from the girl for long. He walks on further, stops again, turns, hesitates a moment, and then bolts straight to her and sticks his nose into the rough wool of the dress that covers her lap. A small cloud drifts across the sun. The girl gasps, recovers her self-possession, and starts feeling the soft wet nose of the antelope. The man waits, fearing that the beast will take fright if he approaches too soon. He hears the wind in the hills as more clouds pile up in the sky. The wind increases and a light snow obscures the sun. The man still waits; the thoughts of a meal of meat and new shoes have faded from his mind in which now is only the tension of the decision as to when to run forward and claim his prey, for the girl is growing restless as the sound of the storm increases. The wind grows stronger; the buck curls up to the girl, fascinated by her yet repelled by the odour of smoke and butter that hangs about her clothes and the braids of her hair. The whole landscape is now dark. The man judges his moment has come, rushes forward and ties a rag around the head of the buck so that the buttery smoky odour of the girl's dress is choked down into him. The girl sits sadly for a moment as the man holds the struggling dying body, then she succumbs to his joking exultation at the thought of the magnificent meal that night.

The sun sets as the meat is being stewed and the skin is stretched out. In the east there is a bank of indigo clouds with longitudinal darker ones set against

them. This fills one-third of the sky. On the south-
west a bank of dull tawny yellow clouds, burning
without heat, covers the sun. In the west this fades
into a cold pale blue sky, set off by a still paler, colder,
more cruel blue, streaked with cirrus clouds of ice,
on the north side of the valley. And between these
two cold cruel blues floats a whole series of high
cottony clouds of every shade of grey, edged with every
shade of dull yellow, while below them the open end
of the valley is now grey, now blue, now almost
green. The earth alone seems warm, for above the
camp the hot springs bubble, and below on the
ground simmer the cooking pots with the stew and
water for buttered tea. The horns of the antelope lie
on the ground before the little black tent; as the grey
and yellow and blue of the sunset fuse into darkness,
the man picks up the horns and places them on a
lha-tho that stands on a spur of rock above the
white sinter of the hot spring. Thus, as that day is
imagined, the scenes of tasting, seeing, touching,
hearing, smelling and apotheosis, transfer themselves
from the tapestries to the dark storm-swept valley,
transforming it into a garden on a summer afternoon,
the mountains closing round to become sun-baked,
fruit-laden walls, within which sit the Unicorn and
the Lady.

"Je la regarday une pose
Elle estoit blanche comme let
Et doulce comme ung aignelet
Vermeilette comme une rose."[7]

The mythology and the drama of the senses fade, remaining in the memory like the end of a dream. The beliefs on which they were based are all but for gotten. Only the landscape and its animal inhabitants persist unchanged, only the hot springs remain to warm a small spot in the cold wind swept valley. Just above the river an icy trickle flows from a patch of snow, still unmelted at the end of July; a little higher up the side of the valley the hot water perennially bubbles into each of the white sintery basins that the springs have built.

The water does not contain the evil smelling and poisonous substances so often found in hot springs, so that, as it cools and becomes aerated, it provides a tropical environment for such warmth loving animals and plants as have made their way across the cold surrounding country. Around the deepest part of one of the basins, where the water is issuing too hot for the hand to be held in it, only submerged sheet like growths of orange bacteria and deep green algae are found. Outside these brilliant sheets of massed cells lies a band of bright green filamentous algae, their threads twisted together to form a floating mat. The water of the outermost part of the basin is pleasantly warm to the touch and is filled with a tangle of water plants, *Chara*, bearing minute orange fruits, and bladderworts with their elaborate traps for micro-scopic animals. Countless water snails, tenuous worms and larvae of salt flies, live in this outer cooler zone. The salt-fly larvae are tough and grotesque grubs with curious forked breathing tubes for tails; they are characteristic inhabitants of hot springs, even though the water be practically fresh, and belong to a family that has invaded other bizarre environments, one species even living in pools of crude petroleum. The water snails are so abundant among the tufts of *Chara* and bladderwort in the warm marginal waters that they seem to crowd one another out of the white sintery basins.

Part of the pasture nearer the river bed is swampy; in places there are small pools of water. These pools, separated from the hot springs by a narrow strip of desert, must receive their water from patches of melting snow. In them water crowsfoot grows, a species of *Ranunculus* that spreads delicate filmy many times divided leaves through the water and holds a small white flower above the surface of the pool. It is a plant of immensely wide distribution. It is certainly found as high in the mountains as is any water plant, but in the swamps of Kashmir it grows in profusion, and its feathery leaves, split into many toes like the feet of a polydactylous bird, gave a name to the same plant growing in quiet ponds and slowly flowing brooks of England. In the lowland waters where the crowsfoot grows, insects, crustacea, snails and small fish may usually be found in abundance. But in the high cold pools in the Chang-chenmo life is very restricted, and, though the edges of the hot springs seem to bubble over with snails, not one can be found living in the swampy pools less than a quarter of a mile away. At a place called Chagra, north-west of Panggong Tso, fresh-water molluscs re-appear, but here again they are found living only in a spring, the water of which is always warm. The same restriction is imposed wherever water snails are found at extreme altitudes, for all the highest records are from thermal springs or from the warm rivulets that flow from them.

The pools that are found at these immense eleva-tions doubtless become solid blocks of ice in the winter, when they do not receive water warmed in the earth. Many sorts of aquatic animals must find it impossible to live under such conditions, and the uplifting of the mountains must have exterminated many of the inhabitants of the waters of their ancient valleys. Hot springs are often found in regions where violent dislocations of the earth's crust have occurred and where one immense mass of rock has slid over another. Thus the very terrestrial forces which were involved in the building of the mountains have provided a few refuges, where one or two of the animals and plants of the country could survive, without having to submit to the violence of the climate around them. As at the bottom of a lake, where a balance between food and oxygen must be achieved before animal life can exist, or on the mountain side where life is controlled by the opposing destructive forces of drought and cold, so in these small refuges a pattern is established, imposing on each pool a design of green and orange. In only one part of the design can animal life flourish, the central region being too hot, the outside world too cold.

Most of the streams of Indian Tibet originate from glaciers and snowfields. In the higher country springs contribute little; most of the water that they produce seeps back into the dry ground. In the lower parts of the valleys, a few clear cold springs issue from cracks in the rocky hillside, to fill little mossy pools, from which streams may descend to join the larger brooks and rivers. These springs must have refreshed many thirsty travellers journeying on the dry road between Leh and the Kashmir valley; they would perhaps have drunk with less pleasure had they known of the zoological riches that such localities contain. Under stones on the floors of these mossy pools and tiny rivulets, dark flatworms rest. They venture out from beneath the pebbles in the evening, but never descend into the larger streams, where the midday sun has warmed the waters. Among the mossy tufts that hang into the water, scarlet water mites are concealed. To the naked eye they appear as minute specks of red among the dark moss fronds, but their minuteness conceals a complexity of structure and a great diversity of form. Several different species can inhabit the moss of a single spring. All the different kinds found in this country are peculiar to it and have never been found outside its cool and running waters.

As the small rivulets flow down the mountains, joining to form larger streams which again discharge their waters into some wide river, perhaps the Indus itself, their inhabitants change, and, as in the lakes and deserts and hot springs, a living pattern is developed. In these running waters the pattern depends on the size of the stream and on the gradient of the valley in which the water flows. In the smallest streams, some mere trickles which flow from the cold and mossy springs, a few little fishes may often be found. These fishes are usually stream loaches, which live habitually among the stones on the bottom, darting powerfully from pool to pool, but apparently unable to make steady progress against the current. Unlike the lake loaches of the Panggong Tso depression, their swim bladders are reduced to mere vestiges enclosed in capsules of bone, so that the stream loaches are not buoyed up in the shallow turbulent water when they leave their homes among the pebbles on the bottom. One of the commonest of the several kinds found in streams is Stoliczka's loach. It is named after its discoverer, the great traveller and geologist Ferdinand Stoliczka, who worked and died in these regions and who is buried behind the garden of the Residency of Leh. Stoliczka's loach has the distinction of reaching greater altitudes than any other kind of fish. It lives in numbers in some of the highest and most barren streams, and may collect in great aggregates, a hundred or more lying huddled together on the bottom of a pool, round some stone, or the waterlogged skull of a mountain sheep.

A curious fish called *Glyptosternon* lives in some of the small streams in the lower valleys. It is a squat and scaleless catfish; the head is grotesquely large and the body tapers from the head, giving to the back of the fish a perfect streamlined profile. The under surface is flat; the margins of the front fins are thickened and ridged, and other ridges are found on its chest. This curious shape enables the fish to retain its hold on the stony bottom of its home, while it affords the least possible resistance to the water that rapidly flows over its back.

As the streams descend from the snows or from springs, they coalesce and grow in size and often in swiftness. They rush through narrow valleys, the walls of which bear patterns of brown and black rocks, contorted in the birth agony of the mountains. A little grass may grow in the bottoms of the valleys; a small gonpa, such as that at Tangtse or at Gya, standing on an isolated rock, may overlook the watercourse. Where the current is not too rapid, a thin film of microscopic plants develops on the surface of the stony bottom, covering it with a greenish or yellowish slime. Green tufts depend from the downstream side of the small boulders that litter the bed of the stream. The light that such green plants must have, if they are to live and grow, easily reaches them through the clear and shallow water.

In these larger mountain brooks the loaches of the head-water streams are still found, but other fish are more common. Two kinds of snow trout are found here, large and powerful fishes belonging to the carp family, but quite unlike the scaly and sluggish carp of lowland waters. One species, the spotted snow trout, has minute and scattered scales on its back, while the other, Stoliczka's snow trout, has lost its scales over almost the whole of its body. The spotted snow trout is the only fish found in the most rapid brooks, where with its horny lips it scrapes such plant growth as it can find off the stones. Stoliczka's snow trout, though apparently unable to live in such torrential streams, can inhabit quiet waters, in which the spotted snow trout is never found. In many places, however, the two live together in the same stream, feeding in the same manner. In spite of the name that English travellers have bestowed on them, these fish are not cold-loving forms. The intensity of the sun in summer may make the water in which they live too warm for a true trout to survive in it, though at night the tenuous atmosphere allows most of the heat to radiate away. Stoliczka's snow trout lays its lemon-yellow eggs in July, so that the young, probably more susceptible to high temperatures than are the adult fish, hatch into a world that is hot in the afternoon though almost at freezing-point at night. Hundreds of snow trout live in the stream of Tangtse, hundreds in the stream that discharges into Panggong Tso. In the mountain

146

brooks that rush down the great fans which flank the Indus, the spotted snow trout is so abundant that sometimes after a flood, when the water recedes from the inundated lower parts of the valleys, the streets of Leh are filled with dying fish. The huge abundance of fish contrasts curiously with the barrenness of the hillsides between which the streams flow; the productiveness of this barren country seems to be concentrated in the streams, just as it is also concentrated in the smaller lakes.

When the mountain brooks reach the Indus, the inhabitants of their waters change with the changing of the landscape through which these waters flow. The river trims the edges of the great fans that bear its tributary streams. These tributaries, led out into innumerable channels, water the living green patches around the villages, the fields of barley and the orchards of apricot trees. The tiny chapels of the smaller valleys are replaced by the huge monastic buildings of Tigtse and Spithug. Rows of white chortens and brown sunburnt mani walls stretch along the roads that link one cultivated patch with another. The river flows now between swampy meadows, now in a narrow rocky gorge, which, however dry and desolate it may appear, has been used as a highway for at least a thousand years.

The spotted snow trout, the most characteristic fish of the mountain brooks, is absent from the deep and turbid waters of the Indus, but a whole series of forms, related to the snow trout yet never found in the clear and shallow tributary streams, now appears. This group of fishes, called the *Schizothoracinae* or hill barbel, lives in all the rivers of Central Asia. About seventy distinct kinds have been recognised, but most of them are so similar to each other that even an ichthyologist finds it hard to distinguish them. They are found in the Pamir mountains, in the streams which unite to produce the Oxus. Several kinds are caught in immense numbers by the fishermen of Lake Issyk-kul. The Indus and its tributaries harbour nearly twenty species; two or three make up most of the catch in the throw nets of the Kashmiri fishermen. In the system of the Upper Brahmaputra, which the Tibetans call Tsang-po before it turns south to break through the Himalayan mountains, there are ten or fifteen species. Some of these live in the main stream, others in the tributaries that drain the country around the golden-roofed temples of Lhasa. Far to the east, on the borders of China, hill barbel live in the upper reaches of the Mekong before it flows among the tropical forests of Burma, and in the head waters of the Yang-tse-kiang and Hwang-ho. A number of species is found in the rivers that flow into the great inland lakes of Central Asia, Lop-nor, Koko-nor, and Balkash.

The basins of these various rivers do not com-municate. Some run to the east, some to the west, collecting their water at first with difficulty from the boundaries of the desert plateau, then more abun-dantly from the encircling snow-covered ranges. Some are carried south, in great gorges cut transversely through the highest of all mountain ranges. Some lose themselves in the desert or discharge their waters into lakes that are too salt for any kind of fish. The *Schizo-thoracinae* are distributed throughout all these different rivers, as if some power had sown their seeds from a height greater than that of the highest mountains, scattering their ancestors throughout an enormous, though definitely circumscribed, area that embraces the source of every Central Asiatic stream. Yet whirl-winds that suck up whole tanks full of fish and frogs, carrying their inhabitants for miles over the Indian plain, so that the Hindu peasants believe that the Elephants of the Lord Indra have drunk from their village water supplies, can hardly provide an explana-tion of this immense distribution. Rains of fishes,[8] though of almost annual occurrence in the tropical and flat regions of Bengal, have never been noticed in Central Asia. The area occupied by the hill barbel is too large, too rugged and for the most part too dry, to have received its fishes in this violent aerial manner. The solution of the mystery must be sought in a different direction.

Small changes in the pattern of the head-water streams may have provided the channels by which the snow trout spread from one river to another, travelling from the Pamirs to Nepal. On the damper side of a mountain range, the streams will receive more water than on the drier slope and will cut back into the rock more rapidly. Finally a stream may eat its way through some pass until it captures the head waters of the valley on the far side. Such an occurrence must often enable the fishes of mountain brooks to spread to new homes.

But a grander event must be sought to account for the spread of the fishes that live in large rivers, and to explain the similarity of the inhabitants of the Indus and the Tsang-po. The flat-edged shoulders of the Chang-chenmo mountains, where butterflies circle around pinnacles of rock, suggest the nature of this occurrence, though they lie aridly in the air, far above the homes of the few fishes that inhabit the stream below. Such flat ridges represent the levels of the valley floors before the last upward movements of the mountains. They can be traced over a large area and their altitude is found to increase toward the west. The streams that flowed in these valleys must have run toward the east, in the opposite direction to the present flow of the Chang-chenmo river. The remains of such valley floors may be found throughout Indian Tibet. They all record the same history. All the rivers of the land ran toward the Tibetan plateau; the Indus valley itself must once have held a river that joined the Tsang-po or Upper Brahmaputra. North of this gigantic stream, others ran through regions that now are desert. Down these rivers the hill barbel could have swum, only impeded in their progress when they reached the sluggish lower reaches, where they would find other and quite unrelated fishes already in possession of the water.

Not until quite recent times, when the mountains rose high enough to cut off the rain from the inner deserts of Central Asia, were the more northern of these streams dried up. Then, across the ever-growing Himalaya, gorges were cut, deepened by earthquakes and the rush of water down steep new slopes. These gorges broke through the mountains, draining away the waters of the older rivers. In this manner erosion and earth movements have moulded the pattern of the present Indus, and have cut out the path up which the traveller enters the western confines of Tibet, and down which he must return.

The imagination is most accurately stimulated by familiar things. As the sun beats down between the dry cliffs of the Indus, where the fishes so curiously proclaim the history of the river, a horse slowly swings along a rocky path, and the mind floats like a boat borne from the mountains on the glitter of the river, through a world of light, and so carries the now familiar memories of all that has been seen, as its cargo. Coral and turquoise and the strings of cowries hanging at the hips of the women, blue and green lakes and the red specks that swim in them, small shells living in the half-airless waters of their depths, or lying dead on their shores, stranded white and half-fossilised, the memorials of a more favoured time; all these, though left behind, are mentally carried down the river, filling the sunlight with the pattern of their dance. At Leh, in the minds of the missionaries from Goa, the Virgin may once have smiled from her mirror; north and east, no longer honoured as the mother of God, her name may have travelled with the Nestorians who cut the white crosses on the rock at Tangtse. At the edge of the plateau, her shadow may once have troubled the *Pantholops*; farther into the desert, among blue basins of wind-tossed water, as yet half-known, the antelope, now in the distance again becoming a magic and mythological creature, exalts his horn and seeks out his doe, coursing over the short tufts of *Artemisia*, through a land where the Virgin has never been, a land that is his inheritance. These memories and these images are borne down on the glittering water from the lakes and mountains, worlds of form replacing ill-spelt names on a map; all this is carried down the river to be recreated in written words and speech and pictures, so that from these places, for a brief time in this life, the spirit may be made flesh.

IV

NOTES

NOTES

SPAIN AT SEA

1, *p.* 6. The Spanish mirror (seventeenth to eighteenth centuries), the statuette of Daphne (by Wenzel Jammitzer of Nuremburg; sixteenth century), and the well-known tapestries of the Lady and the Unicorn (French, fifteenth century) are in the Musée de Cluny, Paris.

2, *p.* 10. Francesco-Emanuele Cagniamila was born at Palermo in 1702 and died there in 1763. The first edition of the *Embryologia Sacra* was published in that city in 1745. A number of subsequent editions and translations appeared. The one used in the preparation of this account is the French abridgment of l'Abbé Dinouard (2nd ed.), 1774.

3, *p.* 12. From Thomas Weelkes' madrigal, *Thule, the Period of Cosmographers.*

4, *pp.* 12, 13. G. Rondeletius, *De Piscibus Marinis*, Lib. XVI, p. 494, Lyons 1554. Marc Éliéser Bloch, *Ichtyologie ou Histoire Naturelle, générale et particulière des Poissons. Avec des Figures enluminées, dessinées d'après nature*, pts I–XII, Berlin 1785–97. Grateful acknowledgment is made to Dr George M. Smith for an opportunity to study Rondeletius and to Dr Jane Oppenheimer for information relating to both works.

5, *p.* 14. The literature on Goa is extensive, but largely ephemeral, and very inaccessible. The following books have been consulted:

D. L. Cottineau de Kloguen, *An Historical Sketch of Goa*, Madras 1831.

J. N. da Fonseca, *An Historical and Archaeological Sketch of the City of Goa*, Bombay 1878.

Caetano Gracias, *Velha Goa*, 2nd ed., Nova Goa 1931.

A. C. G. da Silva Correia, *La Vieille Goa*, Bastoria 1931.

The last author has also published a *Catalogo Bibliografico das Publicações relativas a India Portuguesa, referida a* 31 *de Decembro le* 1930, Nova Goa 1931. This work would have been invaluable if it could have been freely consulted. It was unfortunately out of print in 1932. After considerable difficulties, a copy was located in the National Library "Vasco da Gama" in Panjim, where the book had not even been catalogued. P. M. J. Gabriel de Saldanha, *Historia de Goa*, Nova Goa 1926 (2 vols.) (out of print), gives a good account of the existing remains. None of the recent books add much archaeological material to Fonseca's account, except to indicate what buildings have been destroyed since his time. Correia's *La Vieille Goa*, however, gives excellent photographs of all the important exteriors surviving in the city, and of a few interiors as well. For the cathedral, see:

Luiz Gonçalves, *A Cathedral de Goa*, Boletím da Sociedade de Geographia de Lisboa, Ser. 17 (1898–9), p. 481, Lisboa 1901. (Mainly historical and epigraphical.)

For the history of the Convent of Saint Monica, see:

Frei Agostinho de Santa Maria, *Historia da fundação do Real Convento de Santa Monica na cidade de Goa*, Lisboa 1699.

M. V. de Abreu. *Real Mosteiro de Sta Monica de Goa. Memoria historica*, Nova Goa 1882.

6, *p*. 14. The original cathedral or Sé was founded in 1511 by Diogo Fernandes, acting on the instructions of Albuquerque. The present building, on a different site, was begun some time after 1562; from 1571 onward for a time the architects were Antonio Argueiros and Julio Simão. The body of the church was completed in 1619, the entire building finished in 1631. The retable presumably dates from the beginning of the seventeenth century.

7, *p*. 17. The church of the Bom-Jesus was begun in 1594.

8, *p.* 18. The letter quoted is given in translation by A. Soares (for Bombay Catholic Welfare Organisation), *Souvenir of the Exposition of St Francis Xavier*, Bombay 1922.

9, *p.* 18. The Convent of Saint Monica was founded in 1606, and completed in 1627. It was the second largest in the Portuguese empire at the time of its foundation, but the immense eighteenth-century monastery of Mafra now overshadows all the other convents of that country. Between the time of its foundation and dissolution (1627–1834) six hundred and sixty-one nuns entered the convent.

10, *p.* 18. A number of small buildings that date from before the Spanish Usurpation are still standing, but the Manueline west entrance of S. Francisco (1521) is the only work left from the early part of the sixteenth century that is at all distinctive. The chapels of Saint Catherine (1550), of Saint Francis Xavier (1546) and of Saint Anthony (first half sixteenth century) have been largely or entirely reconstructed; the churches of Nossa Senhora de Monte (prior to 1557) and N. S. de Rosario (first half sixteenth century) were closed in 1932, but appear to be uninteresting. S. Pedro was founded before 1543, but the pulpit is undoubtedly later.

11, *p.* 21. On the ceiling of the second storey of the cloister, there is another gothic-looking painting, of the Tree of Jesse. This subject was evidently popular in Goa, for it also appears in certain ivory carvings. (O. M. Dalton, *Ivory Carvings of the Christian Era*, vol. I, no. 561, p. 171, British Museum, London 1909; Sir Charles Robinson, *Proc. Soc. Antiq. Lond.* vol. XII, p. 267, 1888.) For the importation of prints from the Low Countries into India, see Sir Edward Maclagan, *The Jesuits and the Great Mogul*, chap. XV, London 1932.

12, *p.* 22. For the flying saints, see Norman Douglas, *Old Calabria*.

13, *p.* 23. In spite of the kindness of Padre Trajanus F. Michaele, who provided a scaffolding, no really good photograph of the *pietà* in S. Pedro could be obtained, as the picture is greatly in need of cleaning, and the church rather dark. Professor Theodore Sizer of Yale University, who has examined the rather unsatis-factory prints obtained, thinks that the picture may have been painted in Goa. The late seventeenth-century artist who decorated the choir of S. Francisco must have been familiar with this painting or its prototype.

14, *p.* 26. The church of S. Domingos (1550–64) was destroyed between 1841 and 1865 (Fonseca). No illustrations of it appear to exist.

15, *p.* 27. The church of S. Francisco, founded in 1521, was, except for the west door, entirely rebuilt in 1661. It is thus the latest surviving work of any importance in the city. The Convent of S. João de Deus, of which the remains are of no architectural interest, is even later (1685).

16, *p.* 28. The superiority of the wood sculpture to the other arts of Goa is most striking. Familiarity with material may have in part determined this, for M. Dieulafoy (*Ars Una: Species Mille. Art in Spain and Portugal*, pp. 341–2, London 1912) says that Goan woods were chiefly used by the Portuguese carvers of the seventeenth century. Moreover, examples of ecclesiastical wood sculpture to serve as models were less easily imported than repro-ductions of paintings; the effect of one or two good workmen would be far healthier than that of innumerable inferior copies. Professor Theodore Sizer, who has most kindly examined photo-graphs of the wood sculpture and painting of Goa, has pointed out that excellence in wood sculpture is characteristic of maritime cultures.

17, *p.* 29. The province of Ponda was added to Portuguese India as part of the "Novas Conquistas" in 1795 (F. C. Danvers, *The Portuguese in India*, vol. II, pp. 450–1, London 1894). In these new conquests, religious liberty was guaranteed, and the erection of Hindu temples, long forbidden in Goa, was permitted. The name Manyesha cannot be found on any map; the temple lies just east of the road from Goa to Ponda, a little north of Mardol. It is probably the Malsá temple at Mardol, mentioned by Lopes Mendes (*O Oriente e a America. Memoria apresentada á x sessão do Cong. internac. Orientalistas*, p. 67, Lisboa 1892). The name of the site of the third temple was transcribed as Bandola, but is certainly the Bandordem of the maps. For Gemelli Careri's account, see Churchill's *Voyages*, vol. IV, book XI, chap. I, p. 228, London 1704.

18, *p.* 29. The inscription over the arch that leads into the avenue at Manyesha is, according to Professor Franklin Edgerton of Yale University, meaningless, save for the initial word *Shri*. It may have formed part of a large inscription on an earlier building.

19, *p.* 36. The description of the ladies arriving at church is based on that of F. Pyrard (*Voyage*, vol. II, pt I, pp. 102–3, Hakluyt Society, London 1887). Pyrard visited Goa in 1608, before the cathedral was complete. If any anachronism is inherent in the description of their costumes, it may be pardoned in default of information as to what was worn in Goa twenty-five years later. F. Caroso, in *Nobilità di Dame*, Venice 1605 (?), is said to give detailed instructions as to the method of wearing chopines. (See E. Rodocanachi, *La Femme Italienne à l'Époque de la Renaissance*, Paris 1907.)

20, *p.* 41. See Maclagan, *loc. cit.* chap. XIX; Desideri, who reached Leh in 1715, was the first European to visit the country described in the second part of this book.

PAINTINGS ON A FAN

1, *p.* 48. The spelling of Tibetan names and other words has raised considerable difficulties. On account of the numerous mute prefixes and compound consonants, literal transcriptions often look clumsy, and are frequently misleading. Place names that can be found on maps have been given in a form recognisable to the ear and, as far as possible, also recognisable from the maps of the Survey of India, in which, however, the spelling is usually so incorrect that in few cases can it be used unchanged.

The most complete account of the archaeology of Indian Tibet (Ladak and Rupshu) is given in A. H. Francke, "Antiquities of Indian Tibet", pts I, II, *Arch. Surv. India*, New Imperial Ser. XXXVIII, L, Calcutta 1914, 1926. This work has been invaluable.

The most accessible and complete work on lamaism still seems to be that of L. A. Waddell, *The Buddhism of Tibet or Lamaism*, 2nd ed. (text unrevised), Cambridge 1934.

2, *p.* 51. *berag.* For beliefs connecting the turquoise head-dress with water, see Sarat Chandra Das, *A Tibetan-English Dictionary*, Calcutta 1902.

3, *p.* 55. This discussion is partly influenced by the writings of Sir Grafton Elliot Smith.

4, *p.* 58. A supposed representation of a Bon priest from Lamayuru is given by Francke (*loc. cit.* pt I, pl. XLI).

5, *p.* 59. *Jo-mo*, nun or lady. Here used to indicate a woman, whatever her status, when dressed in a red robe and a cap, like those worn by lamas, and probably the concubine (*ani*) of a lama (S. C. Das, *J. Proc. Asiat. Soc. Bengal* (n.s.), I, p. 106).

6, *p.* 62. Sarat Chandra Das (*Dictionary*, Preface, pp. viii–ix): "With the opening of the 15th century...Tibetan Scholars took largely to the study of Chinese literature, marking the second period of Tibetan literary history, separating the Classical period, when Sanskrit literature served as a model, and the more modern period." A similar division can doubtless be made in the history of Tibetan painting. The best Tibetan work showing Chinese influence appears to have been done at the end of the seventeenth and during the first few years of the eighteenth century. (J. Hackin in *The Influences of Indian Art*, pp. 137–9, The Indian Society, London 1925.)

7, *p.* 69. Francke, *loc. cit.* pt I, pp. 89–90; and *A History of Western Tibet,* p. 51, London 1907, where a Tibetan work *Padma-bka-btan* is given as the authority for the history of the foundation of the gonpa.

8, *p.* 75. The service described may be "*skan-shags* with one hundred and eight lamps" (Waddell, *loc. cit.* p. 221).

9, p. 78. Sir Charles Bell, *The Religion of Tibet*, p. 48, Oxford 1934 *(by permission)*.

10, *p.* 86. The liturgy of the life-giving sacrament is given in translation by Waddell (*loc. cit.* pp. 444–9). Owing to the crowd, some details, including the administering of the wine, could not be observed at Hemis. The end of the ritual on the second day was not seen. According to another visitor present, the image to be cut up was represented as lying prostrate and placed in a triangle chalked on the floor. Whether the trussed image is used only at the ceremonies of the twelfth year, whether its conical hat is really the red hat of the pandits, and whether the entire ritual does not present the periodic killing of a divine ruler, are questions that must be left unanswered. A comparable account of the dances of the morning of the first day has been given by H. H. Godwin-Austin, *Journ. Asiatic Soc. Bengal*, XXXIV, pt I, p. 171, 1866, to which is appended a translation by H. A. Jaeschke of the "Dance Book of the 10th" (day of the 5th month). Unfortunately the technical terms and some other matters are omitted as untranslatable, and the account throws little light on the problems of the festival. The identification of one of the dancers as Shakya-muni is tentative.

11, *p.* 91. The name of this local deity is doubtful. It was written by a lama in Miru as Cho-mo-kya-mar. In the small villages, even the lamas are apt to spell incorrectly.

LAKES IN THE DESERT

1, *p.* **99.** Most of the material of this section has been published in the scientific results of the Yale North India Expedition, in the *Memoirs of the Connecticut Academy of Arts and Sciences,* vols. VIII–X (1934–6). Grateful acknowledgment is made to Dr L. H. Hyman, Dr M. Ueno, Dr O. Lundblad and Dr S. L. Hora, whose articles have been used, to Dr E. D. Merrill, formerly Director of the New York Botanic Garden, who determined specimens of the plants mentioned; to Dr A. Avinoff who determined the butter⁄flies described on p. 133, and particularly to Dr H. de Terra, whose brilliant physiographic studies (*Geograph. Rev.* vol. XXIV, p. 12, 1934) have provided a basis for the interpretation of the distribution of fishes given on pp. 150–1.

2, *p.* **107.** For the Kargil artifact, see J. and C. Hawkes and H. de Terra, *Mem. Conn. Acad. Art. Sci.* vol. VIII, p. 1, 1933.

3, *p.* **108.** See H. A. Francke, *Sitz. Ber. d. preuss. Akad. Wiss. phil.⁄hist. Kl.* p. 366, Berlin 1925, and F. W. K. Müller, *ibid.* p. 371. For information as to the hitherto⁄unpublished Tokharian inscription, grateful acknowledgment is made to M. E. Benveniste and Professor Silvain Levi. For the history of the Panggong Complex, see H. de Terra, *Geograph. Rev.* vol. XXIV, p. 12, 1934, and H. de Terra and G. E. Hutchinson, *Geograph. Journ.* vol. LXXXIV, p. 311, 1934.

4, *p.* **124.** Sir Thomas Browne, *Hydriotaphia, Urne⁄Burial,* chap. I.

5, *p.* **133.** The highest recorded terrestrial animals are spiders, found at an altitude of 22,000 ft. in the Mount Everest region; see R. W. G. Hingston, *Geograph. Journ.* vol. LXV, p. 185, 1925.

6, *p.* **135.** This version of the unicorn legend is given by Col. R. Meinertzhagen (*Geograph. Journ.* vol. LXX, p. 129, 1927) who states that he was told it in the Chang-chenmo. The story was unknown in Phobrang in 1932. The familiar mediaeval mythology of the unicorn is found in *Physiologus* and is presumably of oriental origin. See also W. R. Dawson and F. Kingdon Ward, *Proc. Linn. Soc. London*, pp. 41–6, 1934–5.

7, *p.* 139. From the fifteenth-century song *L'Amour de moy*; the words and melody both express the *hortus inclusus* as perfectly as do the tapestries in the Cluny.

8, *p.* 149. For rains of fishes in India, see S. L. Hora, *Journ. and Proc. Asiatic Soc. Bengal* (n.s.), vol. XXIX, p. 95, 1933.

V
INDEX

INDEX

(Numbers in heavy type refer to Notes)

INDEX

For EU product safety concerns, contact us at Calle de José Abascal, 56–1°, 28003 Madrid, Spain or eugpsr@cambridge.org.

www.ingramcontent.com/pod-product-compliance
Ingram Content Group UK Ltd.
Pitfield, Milton Keynes, MK11 3LW, UK
UKHW012344130625
459647UK00009B/530